Flask Fundamentals for API Development

Imagine building a dynamic weather app that retrieves data from external sources, or a social media platform that connects users seamlessly.

Katie Millie

Flask Fundamentals for API Development

Imagine building a dynamic weather app that retrieves data from external sources, or a social media platform that connects users seamlessly.

By

Katie Millie

Copyright notice

Copyright © 2024 Katie Millie. All rights reserved.

This digital domain, along with all its contents, stands as the exclusive intellectual creation of Katie Millie. Redistribution or reproduction, whether in whole or in part, in any manner, is strictly prohibited without explicit written consent.

Without our prior written authorization, you are prohibited from disseminating or exploiting the content for commercial purposes. Additionally, transmitting or storing it within any other electronic retrieval system or website is strictly prohibited.

Unauthorized utilization of this website may result in legal action, including claims for damages and potential criminal charges.

From the vibrant strokes of creativity to the meticulously constructed prose, every facet of this online platform reflects Katie Millie's unwavering commitment and fervor. As you navigate through these digital realms, take note that each pixel, each sentence, encapsulates the very essence of Katie's imagination.

Your acknowledgment and respect for the creative pursuits manifested within this virtual space are deeply appreciated. Together, let us cultivate a culture that values and safeguards intellectual property rights.

Table of Contents

INTRODUCTION

Chapter 1

    The Rise of the Connected World: A Journey through Flask API Development

        Demystifying APIs: The Secret Sauce of Integration with Flask

            Why Flask? The Lightweight Champion for API Development

Chapter 2

    Foundations of Web Development - Setting the Stage for Flask

        Understanding Requests and Responses: The Language of the Web

            Flask's Role in the Web Development Symphony

Chapter 3

    Getting Started with Flask - Your First Steps into the API Dojo

        Creating Your First Flask Application: Hello, World (API Style)!

            Running and Testing Your Flask App: Debugging Like a Pro

Chapter 4

    Crafting Powerful Endpoints - The Gates to Your API Kingdom

        HTTP Methods Demystified: GET, POST, PUT, and DELETE Explained

            Building Dynamic Endpoints with Flask

- Routing: URL Magic

Chapter 5
- Data Wrangling with Flask - Taming the Data Flow
  - Working with JSON: The Universal Language of APIs
    - Handling User Input with Flask Request Objects: Extracting Data with Ease
      - Sending Responses Back: Returning Data to the User

Chapter 6
- Error Handling and Validation - Building a Robust API Fortress
  - Crafting Informative Error Messages: User-Friendly Troubleshooting
    - Data Validation: Safeguarding Your API from Bad Data
      - Techniques for Input Validation: Ensuring Data Integrity

Chapter 7
- Testing Your Masterpiece - Building Confidence in Your API
  - Setting Up a Testing Framework: Tools for Flask API Development
    - Writing Unit Tests for Flask Applications: Ensuring Flawless Functionality

Chapter 8
- Building a Dynamic Weather App with Flask - Consuming External Data
  - Building a Flask API to Fetch Weather Information
    - Displaying Weather Data on a User Interface

using Flask

Chapter 9

Creating a Simple Social Media Platform - Connecting Users with Flask

Building Endpoints for User Interaction: Posting and Sharing Content with Flask

Exploring Authentication Techniques: Securing Your Social Network with Flask

Chapter 10

Deployment Strategies - Sharing Your API with the World

Configuration for Deployment: Optimizing Your API for Production with Flask

Monitoring and Maintaining Your API: Keeping Your Creation Alive with Flask

Conclusion

Appendix

Exploring Common Flask Libraries and Extensions for API Development

INTRODUCTION

Flask Fundamentals for API Development: Unleash the Python Powerhouse Within

Have you ever dreamt of building the next big software sensation? Perhaps an app that seamlessly integrates with other services, or a website that communicates with lightning speed? The secret weapon to achieving this lies in the realm of APIs (Application Programming Interfaces). But venturing into this exciting world can feel daunting, like trying to decipher ancient scrolls. Fear not, fellow coder! "**Flask Fundamentals for API Development**" is your Rosetta Stone, ready to crack the code and unlock the magic of Flask, Python's API development powerhouse.

This book isn't your average, dry technical manual. We'll ditch the sleep-inducing jargon and dive into a whirlwind of practical knowledge, all presented in a way that's both informative and engaging. Imagine yourself as a code samurai, wielding the power of Flask with elegance and precision. With each chapter, you'll hone your skills, conquering new challenges and building your very own arsenal of API-building techniques.

But why Flask? In a world brimming with frameworks, Flask stands out as the sleek katana to the clunky broadsword. It's lightweight, incredibly versatile, and lets you focus on the core functionality of your API without getting bogged down in unnecessary complexity. Whether you're a seasoned Python developer or a curious newcomer, Flask offers a smooth learning curve that empowers you to create robust and scalable APIs in record time.

This book is your comprehensive guide to mastering Flask for API development. We'll embark on a thrilling journey that covers:

- **The Foundations of Flask:** We'll start by setting the stage, understanding the core concepts of web development and APIs. You'll learn how Flask fits into the grand scheme of things, and we'll establish a solid foundation for building upon.
- **Crafting Endpoints:** Endpoints are the beating heart of your API, the designated ports through which data flows. We'll delve into the art of crafting powerful endpoints, using Python's magic to handle various HTTP requests (GET, POST, PUT, DELETE) with finesse.
- **Data Wrangling with Flask:** APIs are all about data exchange. This book will equip you with the tools to handle incoming and outgoing data like a pro. We'll explore techniques for data serialization (converting data into a transmittable format) using popular libraries like JSON.
- **Error Handling and Validation:** No API is perfect, and errors are inevitable. But fear not! We'll equip you with the knowledge to gracefully handle errors, providing informative messages to both you and the users of your API. Additionally, we'll explore robust validation techniques to ensure only the right kind of data enters your system.

- **Testing Your Masterpiece:** A well-tested API is a reliable API. We'll delve into the world of unit testing, a powerful technique to ensure each component of your API functions flawlessly. By the end, you'll have the confidence to unleash your creation upon the world!

This book isn't just about technical prowess; it's about empowering you to bring your ideas to life. We'll explore real-world examples to showcase the practical applications of Flask APIs. Imagine building a dynamic weather app that retrieves data from external sources, or a social media platform that connects users seamlessly. The possibilities are endless!

"**Flask Fundamentals for API Development**" is more than just a book; it's your launchpad into the exciting world of API development. With its clear explanations, captivating examples, and practical exercises, you'll be crafting powerful APIs in no time. So, grab your metaphorical katana (or your favorite coding device), and let's embark on this thrilling adventure together!

Chapter 1

The Rise of the Connected World: A Journey through Flask API Development

In the digital age, connectivity has become the cornerstone of modern society. From smartphones to smart cities, the world is increasingly interconnected, thanks to advancements in technology. In this essay, we will explore the rise of the connected world and delve into the fundamentals of Flask API development, a powerful tool for building web applications that fuel this connectivity.

The Rise of the Connected World:

The connected world encompasses various aspects of our daily lives, from communication and entertainment to healthcare and transportation. With the proliferation of internet-enabled devices, individuals can now seamlessly interact with each other and their surroundings like never before. This interconnectedness has led to a revolution in how we live, work, and play.

One of the driving forces behind the rise of the connected world is the Internet of Things (IoT). IoT devices, ranging from wearable fitness trackers to home automation systems, gather data and communicate with each other over the internet. This interconnected network of devices enables the automation of tasks, optimization of processes, and enhancement of user experiences.

Another key component of the connected world is the proliferation of mobile devices. Smartphones and tablets have become ubiquitous, serving as our gateway to the digital realm. With mobile apps, users can access a wealth of information and services on the go, staying connected to the world around them no matter where they are.

Furthermore, advancements in cloud computing have played a significant role in enabling connectivity on a global scale. Cloud platforms provide the infrastructure and resources necessary to support the vast network of connected devices and services. With the cloud, data can be stored, processed, and accessed from anywhere, facilitating real-time communication and collaboration.

Flask API Development:

At the heart of the connected world are web applications that facilitate communication and data exchange between devices and services. Flask, a lightweight and versatile web framework for Python, is a popular choice for building APIs that power these applications. With Flask, developers can quickly create robust and scalable APIs to serve data and handle requests from clients.

To demonstrate the fundamentals of Flask API development, let's create a simple API for managing a todo list application. We'll start by setting up a basic Flask project structure and defining routes for handling CRUD (Create, Read, Update, Delete) operations on todo items.

```python
from flask import Flask, jsonify, request

app = Flask(__name__)

# Sample todo list data
todos = [
    { 'id': 1, 'title': 'Learn Flask', 'completed': False },
    { 'id': 2, 'title': 'Build API', 'completed': False }
]

# Route to get all todos
@app.route('/todos', methods=['GET'])
def get_todos():
    return jsonify(todos)

# Route to add a new todo
@app.route('/todos', methods=['POST'])
```

```python
def add_todo():
    new_todo = request.json
    todos.append(new_todo)
    return jsonify(new_todo), 201

# Route to update a todo
@app.route('/todos/<int:todo_id>', methods=['PUT'])
def update_todo(todo_id):
    todo = next((todo for todo in todos if todo['id'] == todo_id), None)
    if todo:
        todo.update(request.json)
        return jsonify(todo)
    else:
        return jsonify({'error': 'Todo not found'}), 404

# Route to delete a todo
@app.route('/todos/<int:todo_id>', methods=['DELETE'])
def delete_todo(todo_id):
    global todos
    todos = [todo for todo in todos if todo['id'] != todo_id]
    return '', 204

if __name__ == '__main__':
    app.run(debug=True)
```
'''

In this example, we define routes for retrieving all todos, adding a new todo, updating a todo, and deleting a todo. Each route corresponds to a specific HTTP method (GET, POST, PUT, DELETE) and performs the corresponding CRUD operation on the todo list.

The rise of the connected world has transformed the way we live, work, and interact with our environment. From IoT devices to mobile apps, connectivity has become ingrained in every aspect of our daily lives. As we continue to embrace this interconnected future, tools like Flask API development will play a crucial role in building the infrastructure that powers the connected world. With Flask, developers have the flexibility and power to create robust APIs that enable seamless communication and data exchange between devices and services, driving innovation and shaping the future of technology.

Demystifying APIs: The Secret Sauce of Integration with Flask

In today's digital landscape, APIs (Application Programming Interfaces) serve as the backbone of modern software development and integration. From social media platforms to e-commerce websites, APIs enable seamless communication and data exchange between different applications and systems. In this essay, we will demystify APIs and explore how Flask, a lightweight web framework for Python, facilitates API development, using code examples to illustrate key concepts.

Understanding APIs:

At its core, an API is a set of rules and protocols that allows different software applications to communicate with each other. It defines how requests and responses should be structured, what data can be accessed or manipulated, and what actions can be performed. APIs abstract away the complexity of underlying systems, enabling developers to interact with them in a standardized and predictable manner.

There are various types of APIs, including:

1. RESTful APIs: Representational State Transfer (REST) is a popular architectural style for designing networked applications. RESTful APIs use HTTP methods (GET, POST, PUT, DELETE) to perform CRUD operations on resources, and they typically communicate using JSON or XML.

2. SOAP APIs: Simple Object Access Protocol (SOAP) is a protocol for exchanging structured information in the implementation of web services. SOAP APIs use XML for message formatting and support advanced features like security and transactionality.

3. GraphQL APIs: GraphQL is a query language for APIs that enables clients to request only the data they need. Unlike RESTful APIs, which expose fixed endpoints, GraphQL APIs allow clients to define their queries and retrieve nested data in a single request.

Flask Fundamentals for API Development:

Flask is a lightweight and flexible web framework for Python, ideal for building APIs due to its simplicity and extensibility. Let's explore the fundamentals of Flask API development by creating a simple RESTful API for managing a bookstore.

```python
from flask import Flask, jsonify, request

app = Flask(__name__)

# Sample bookstore data
books = [
    {"id": 1, "title": "Python Programming", "author": "Guido van Rossum", "year": 1991},
```

    {"id": 2, "title": "Flask Essentials", "author": "Shalabh Aggarwal", "year": 2018}
]

```python
# Route to get all books
@app.route('/books', methods=['GET'])
def get_books():
    return jsonify(books)

# Route to get a specific book by ID
@app.route('/books/<int:book_id>', methods=['GET'])
def get_book(book_id):
    book = next((book for book in books if book['id'] == book_id), None)
    if book:
        return jsonify(book)
    else:
        return jsonify({"error": "Book not found"}), 404

# Route to add a new book
@app.route('/books', methods=['POST'])
def add_book():
    new_book = request.json
    books.append(new_book)
    return jsonify(new_book), 201

# Route to update an existing book
@app.route('/books/<int:book_id>', methods=['PUT'])
```

```python
def update_book(book_id):
    book = next((book for book in books if book['id'] == book_id), None)
    if book:
        book.update(request.json)
        return jsonify(book)
    else:
        return jsonify({"error": "Book not found"}), 404

# Route to delete a book
@app.route('/books/<int:book_id>', methods=['DELETE'])
def delete_book(book_id):
    global books
    books = [book for book in books if book['id'] != book_id]
    return '', 204

if __name__ == '__main__':
    app.run(debug=True)
```
```

In this Flask application, we define routes for handling CRUD operations on a collection of books. The `/books` route supports GET (retrieve all books) and POST (add a new book) methods, while the `/books/<int:book_id>` route supports GET (retrieve a specific book), PUT
```

(update an existing book), and DELETE (delete a book) methods.

APIs are the secret sauce that powers integration and interoperability in the digital age. By providing standardized interfaces for communication and data exchange, APIs enable developers to build complex systems that leverage the capabilities of multiple applications and services. With Flask, developers have a powerful tool for creating APIs that are flexible, scalable, and easy to maintain. By understanding the fundamentals of API development and leveraging the capabilities of frameworks like Flask, developers can unlock new possibilities for innovation and collaboration in the world of software development.

Why Flask? The Lightweight Champion for API Development

In the realm of web development, choosing the right framework can make all the difference in terms of productivity, scalability, and performance. Flask, a lightweight and versatile web framework for Python, has emerged as a popular choice for API development due to its simplicity, flexibility, and extensive ecosystem. In this essay, we will explore the reasons why Flask stands out as the champion for API development, backed by code examples that illustrate its fundamental principles.

1. Simplicity and Minimalism:

Flask prides itself on its simplicity and minimalist design. Unlike heavyweight frameworks that come bundled with a plethora of features and dependencies, Flask provides only the essentials, allowing developers to build applications without being bogged down by unnecessary complexity.

```python
from flask import Flask

app = Flask(__name__)

@app.route('/')
def hello_world():
    return 'Hello, Flask!'
```

In just a few lines of code, we can create a basic Flask application that responds with "Hello, Flask!" when accessed at the root URL. This simplicity makes Flask ideal for getting started quickly and focusing on the task at hand without getting overwhelmed by boilerplate code.

2. Flexibility and Extensibility:

While Flask may be lightweight, it is by no means lacking in flexibility or extensibility. Flask follows the "microframework" philosophy, which means it provides the core components needed to build web applications while allowing developers to add additional functionality as needed through extensions.

```python
from flask import Flask
from flask_sqlalchemy import SQLAlchemy

app = Flask(__name__)
app.config['SQLALCHEMY_DATABASE_URI'] = 'sqlite:///example.db'
db = SQLAlchemy(app)

class User(db.Model):
    id = db.Column(db.Integer, primary_key=True)
    username = db.Column(db.String(80), unique=True, nullable=False)
    email = db.Column(db.String(120), unique=True, nullable=False)

    def __repr__(self):
        return '<User %r>' % self.username
```

In this example, we integrate Flask with SQLAlchemy, a popular ORM (Object-Relational Mapping) library for database interaction. By leveraging Flask extensions, we can easily add features such as database connectivity and ORM capabilities to our application, without reinventing the wheel.

3. Powerful Routing System:

One of Flask's most notable features is its powerful routing system, which allows developers to map URLs to Python functions with ease. Routes can be defined using decorators, making it intuitive to define the behavior of different parts of the application.

```python
from flask import Flask

app = Flask(__name__)

@app.route('/')
def index():
    return 'Home Page'

@app.route('/about')
def about():
    return 'About Page'
```

```
@app.route('/user/<username>')
def profile(username):
    return f'Hello, {username}!'
```

In this example, we define three routes: `/` for the home page, `/about` for the about page, and `/user/<username>` for user profiles. Flask automatically extracts variables from the URL and passes them as arguments to the corresponding functions, making it easy to access dynamic data.

4. Built-in Development Server:

Flask comes with a built-in development server, making it convenient to test and debug applications locally without the need for additional setup. The development server automatically reloads the application when changes are detected, allowing for a smooth and efficient development workflow.

```python
if __name__ == '__main__':
    app.run(debug=True)
```

By adding this conditional statement at the end of the script, we can run the Flask application using the built-in development server with debugging enabled. This enables real-time feedback and helps identify and fix issues quickly during development.

Flask's simplicity, flexibility, and powerful features make it the lightweight champion for API development. Whether you're building a small-scale prototype or a large-scale production application, Flask provides the tools and infrastructure needed to get the job done efficiently. By harnessing the power of Flask and its extensive ecosystem of extensions, developers can create robust and scalable APIs that meet the demands of today's interconnected world.

Chapter 2

Foundations of Web Development - Setting the Stage for Flask

The Web in Action: Clients, Servers, and the HTTP Dance

The World Wide Web has become an integral part of our daily lives, enabling seamless communication, information sharing, and collaboration on a global scale. At the heart of the web's functionality are clients and servers, which engage in a dance of HTTP requests and responses to deliver content and services to users. In this essay, we will explore the inner workings of the web, dissecting the roles of clients and servers, and diving into the intricacies of the HTTP protocol. Along the way, we'll utilize Flask, a lightweight web framework for Python, to illustrate key concepts and demonstrate the principles of web development.

Understanding Clients and Servers:

At its core, the web operates on a client-server model, where clients and servers communicate with each other to exchange data and fulfill requests. Clients, such as web browsers or mobile apps, initiate requests for resources or services, while servers, which host websites and applications, respond to these requests by providing the requested content.

When a user enters a URL into a web browser or clicks on a link, the browser acts as a client and sends an HTTP request to the appropriate server. The server processes the request, retrieves the requested resource, and sends an HTTP response back to the client, which then renders the content for the user to view.

HTTP: The Language of the Web:

HTTP (Hypertext Transfer Protocol) is the foundation of communication on the World Wide Web. It defines a set of rules and conventions for how clients and servers should exchange information, including requests for resources and responses containing the requested content.

HTTP requests typically consist of four main components:

1. Method: The HTTP method (also known as HTTP verb) indicates the action to be performed on the resource. Common HTTP methods include GET (retrieve a resource), POST (submit data to be processed), PUT (update an existing resource), and DELETE (remove a resource).

2. URL: The Uniform Resource Locator (URL) specifies the location of the resource being requested. It consists of a protocol (e.g., http:// or https://), domain name, and optional path and query parameters.

3. Headers: HTTP headers provide additional metadata about the request, such as the user agent, content type, and authentication credentials. Headers help servers understand how to process the request and provide the appropriate response.

4. Body (optional): For certain types of requests, such as POST or PUT, the body contains data to be sent to the server. The body can be formatted using various content types, such as JSON or form-urlencoded data.

```python
import requests

# Example HTTP GET request
response = requests.get('https://api.github.com/users/octocat')
print(response.status_code)  # Print HTTP status code
print(response.json())       # Print JSON response data
```

In this Python code snippet, we use the `requests` library to send an HTTP GET request to the GitHub API, requesting information about the user "octocat". We then print the HTTP status code and the JSON response data returned by the server.

Flask Fundamentals for API Development:

Flask, a lightweight web framework for Python, provides a powerful platform for building web applications and APIs. Let's explore the fundamentals of Flask API development by creating a simple API for managing a todo list.

```python
from flask import Flask, jsonify, request

app = Flask(__name__)

# Sample todo list data
todos = [
    {"id": 1, "task": "Learn Flask", "completed": False},
    {"id": 2, "task": "Build API", "completed": False}
]

# Route to get all todos
@app.route('/todos', methods=['GET'])
def get_todos():
```

```python
    return jsonify(todos)

# Route to get a specific todo by ID
@app.route('/todos/<int:todo_id>', methods=['GET'])
def get_todo(todo_id):
    todo = next((todo for todo in todos if todo['id'] == todo_id), None)
    if todo:
        return jsonify(todo)
    else:
        return jsonify({"error": "Todo not found"}), 404

# Route to add a new todo
@app.route('/todos', methods=['POST'])
def add_todo():
    new_todo = request.json
    todos.append(new_todo)
    return jsonify(new_todo), 201

# Route to update an existing todo
@app.route('/todos/<int:todo_id>', methods=['PUT'])
def update_todo(todo_id):
    todo = next((todo for todo in todos if todo['id'] == todo_id), None)
    if todo:
        todo.update(request.json)
        return jsonify(todo)
    else:
```

```
        return jsonify({"error": "Todo not found"}), 404

# Route to delete a todo
@app.route('/todos/<int:todo_id>', methods=['DELETE'])
def delete_todo(todo_id):
    global todos
    todos = [todo for todo in todos if todo['id'] != todo_id]
    return '', 204

if __name__ == '__main__':
    app.run(debug=True)
```
```

In this Flask application, we define routes for handling CRUD operations on a todo list. The `/todos` route supports GET (retrieve all todos) and POST (add a new todo) methods, while the `/todos/<int:todo_id>` route supports GET (retrieve a specific todo), PUT (update an existing todo), and DELETE (delete a todo) methods.

The web is a dynamic ecosystem driven by the interaction between clients and servers, facilitated by the HTTP protocol. Understanding the roles of clients and servers, as well as the principles of HTTP communication, is essential for building effective web applications and APIs. With Flask, developers have a powerful tool for creating APIs that enable seamless data
```

exchange and integration between different systems and platforms. By mastering the fundamentals of Flask API development, developers can unlock the potential of the web and build innovative solutions that shape the future of technology.

Understanding Requests and Responses: The Language of the Web

At the core of the World Wide Web lies the exchange of data between clients and servers. This exchange occurs through HTTP requests and responses, which serve as the language of communication on the web. In this essay, we will delve into the intricacies of HTTP requests and responses, exploring their structure, components, and significance in web development. Throughout our exploration, we will utilize Flask, a lightweight web framework for Python, to illustrate key concepts and demonstrate practical examples of request-response interactions.

Anatomy of an HTTP Request:

HTTP (Hypertext Transfer Protocol) requests are messages sent by clients to request resources from a server. Each HTTP request consists of several components, each serving a specific purpose in the communication process.

1. HTTP Method: The HTTP method (also known as HTTP verb) indicates the action to be performed on the resource identified by the URL. Common HTTP methods include GET, POST, PUT, DELETE, among others.

2. URL: The Uniform Resource Locator (URL) specifies the location of the resource being requested. It typically consists of a protocol (e.g., http:// or https://), domain name, and optional path and query parameters.

3. Headers: HTTP headers provide additional metadata about the request, such as the user agent, content type, and authentication credentials. Headers help servers understand how to process the request and provide the appropriate response.

4. Body (optional): For certain types of requests, such as POST or PUT, the body contains data to be sent to the server. The body can be formatted using various content types, such as JSON or form-urlencoded data.

Let's examine an example of an HTTP request using Python and the `requests` library:

```python
import requests
```

```
# Example HTTP GET request
response = requests.get('https://api.github.com/users/octocat')
print(response.status_code)  # Print HTTP status code
print(response.json())       # Print JSON response data
```

In this code snippet, we use the `requests` library to send an HTTP GET request to the GitHub API, requesting information about the user "octocat". We then print the HTTP status code and the JSON response data returned by the server.

Anatomy of an HTTP Response:

HTTP responses are messages sent by servers to provide clients with the requested resources or indicate errors or other status information. Like HTTP requests, HTTP responses consist of several components that convey important information about the response.

1. Status Code: The HTTP status code indicates the outcome of the request. Status codes are grouped into five categories, each with its own set of codes: informational (1xx), success (2xx), redirection (3xx), client error (4xx), and server error (5xx).

2. Headers: HTTP response headers provide additional metadata about the response, such as the content type, content length, and caching directives. Headers help clients understand how to interpret the response and handle it appropriately.

3. Body: The body of an HTTP response contains the requested resource or error message, formatted according to the specified content type. Common content types include text/html for HTML documents, application/json for JSON data, and image/png for image files.

Let's examine an example of an HTTP response using Flask:

```python
from flask import Flask, jsonify

app = Flask(__name__)

# Route to return a JSON response
@app.route('/hello')
def hello():
    return jsonify({'message': 'Hello, Flask!'})

if __name__ == '__main__':
    app.run(debug=True)
```

In this Flask application, we define a route `/hello` that returns a JSON response with a simple message. When a client sends an HTTP GET request to this route, the server responds with a JSON object containing the message "Hello, Flask!".

Understanding the HTTP Lifecycle:

The exchange of HTTP requests and responses follows a lifecycle that encompasses several steps:

1. Client Sends Request: A client initiates an HTTP request by sending a request message to the server. The request message includes the HTTP method, URL, headers, and optional body data.

2. Server Receives Request: The server receives the HTTP request and processes it according to the specified URL route and associated handler function. The server may perform tasks such as retrieving data from a database, processing form submissions, or generating dynamic content.

3. Server Sends Response: After processing the request, the server constructs an HTTP response containing the requested resource or an error message. The response message includes the HTTP status code, headers, and body data.

4. Client Receives Response: The client receives the HTTP response and interprets it based on the status code and content type. If the status code indicates success (2xx), the client may render the content for the user to view. If the status code indicates an error or redirection, the client may display an error message or follow the redirection instructions.

5. Connection Closes (Optional): Depending on the connection settings, the connection between the client and server may close after the response is sent. In persistent connections (e.g., HTTP/1.1), the connection remains open for subsequent requests, improving performance by reducing connection overhead.

HTTP requests and responses form the backbone of communication on the World Wide Web, enabling clients and servers to exchange data and resources seamlessly. By understanding the anatomy of HTTP messages and the lifecycle of HTTP communication, developers can build robust web applications and APIs that leverage the power of the web. With tools like Flask, developers have a flexible and powerful framework for building web applications that adhere to the principles of

HTTP communication, facilitating efficient and effective interaction between clients and servers.

Flask's Role in the Web Development Symphony

In the ever-evolving landscape of web development, Flask has emerged as a powerful and versatile framework for building web applications and APIs. With its minimalist design, extensibility, and flexibility, Flask plays a crucial role in orchestrating the symphony of web development, enabling developers to create robust and scalable solutions. In this essay, we will explore Flask's role in the web development ecosystem, delving into its core principles, features, and practical applications. Through code examples and demonstrations of Flask fundamentals for API development, we will showcase the framework's capabilities and illustrate its significance in modern web development.

Understanding Flask:

Flask is a lightweight web framework for Python, designed to be simple, easy to use, and highly extensible. Unlike monolithic frameworks that come bundled with numerous features and dependencies, Flask follows the "microframework" philosophy, providing only the essentials needed to get started with web development.

This minimalist approach makes Flask ideal for building small to medium-sized applications and APIs, where simplicity and flexibility are paramount.

Key Features of Flask:

1. Routing: Flask's routing system allows developers to map URLs to Python functions, making it easy to define the behavior of different parts of the application. Routes are defined using decorators, which specify the URL pattern and HTTP methods associated with each route.

```python
from flask import Flask

app = Flask(__name__)

@app.route('/')
def index():
    return 'Hello, Flask!'

if __name__ == '__main__':
    app.run(debug=True)
```

In this example, we define a route `/` that renders the message "Hello, Flask!" when accessed. The `@app.route('/')` decorator specifies the URL pattern, while the `index()` function defines the behavior of the route.

2. Extensibility: Flask's modular architecture allows developers to extend its functionality through third-party extensions. These extensions provide additional features and integrations, such as database support, authentication, and API documentation. Flask extensions are easy to install and integrate into applications, giving developers the flexibility to add functionality as needed.

```python
from flask import Flask
from flask_sqlalchemy import SQLAlchemy

app = Flask(__name__)
app.config['SQLALCHEMY_DATABASE_URI'] = 'sqlite:///example.db'
db = SQLAlchemy(app)

class User(db.Model):
    id = db.Column(db.Integer, primary_key=True)
    username = db.Column(db.String(80), unique=True, nullable=False)
    email = db.Column(db.String(120), unique=True, nullable=False)

    def __repr__(self):
```

```
        return '<User %r>' % self.username
```

In this example, we integrate Flask with SQLAlchemy, a popular ORM (Object-Relational Mapping) library for database interaction. The `db` object represents the database connection, and the `User` class defines the structure of the `users` table.

3. Jinja2 Templating: Flask uses the Jinja2 template engine to generate dynamic HTML content based on templates. Jinja2 templates allow developers to write HTML with placeholders for dynamic data, which are filled in when the template is rendered. This enables the creation of dynamic web pages with reusable components and flexible data binding.

```html
<!DOCTYPE html>
<html>
<head>
    <title>{{ title }}</title>
</head>
<body>
    <h1>Hello, {{ name }}!</h1>
</body>
</html>
```

In this example, we define a Jinja2 template that renders a personalized greeting message with the name provided as a variable.

Flask's Role in API Development:

Flask's lightweight and flexible nature make it well-suited for building APIs (Application Programming Interfaces) that enable communication between different systems and platforms. Flask's simplicity and extensibility simplify the process of building APIs, allowing developers to focus on defining the API endpoints and business logic without being burdened by unnecessary complexity.

Let's explore the fundamentals of Flask API development by creating a simple API for managing a todo list:

```python
from flask import Flask, jsonify, request

app = Flask(__name__)

# Sample todo list data
todos = [
    {"id": 1, "task": "Learn Flask", "completed": False},
```

    {"id": 2, "task": "Build API", "completed": False}
]

Route to get all todos
@app.route('/todos', methods=['GET'])
def get_todos():
    return jsonify(todos)

Route to get a specific todo by ID
@app.route('/todos/<int:todo_id>', methods=['GET'])
def get_todo(todo_id):
    todo = next((todo for todo in todos if todo['id'] == todo_id), None)
    if todo:
        return jsonify(todo)
    else:
        return jsonify({"error": "Todo not found"}), 404

Route to add a new todo
@app.route('/todos', methods=['POST'])
def add_todo():
    new_todo = request.json
    todos.append(new_todo)
    return jsonify(new_todo), 201

Route to update an existing todo
@app.route('/todos/<int:todo_id>', methods=['PUT'])
def update_todo(todo_id):

```
        todo = next((todo for todo in todos if todo['id'] ==
todo_id), None)
    if todo:
        todo.update(request.json)
        return jsonify(todo)
    else:
        return jsonify({"error": "Todo not found"}), 404

# Route to delete a todo
@app.route('/todos/<int:todo_id>', 
methods=['DELETE'])
def delete_todo(todo_id):
    global todos
    todos = [todo for todo in todos if todo['id'] != todo_id]
    return '', 204

if __name__ == '__main__':
    app.run(debug=True)
```
```

In this Flask application, we define routes for handling CRUD (Create, Read, Update, Delete) operations on a todo list. Each route corresponds to a specific HTTP method and performs the corresponding operation on the todo list data. By leveraging Flask's routing system and request handling capabilities, we can easily create a RESTful API for managing todo items.
```

Flask's role in the web development ecosystem is pivotal, serving as a lightweight and flexible framework for building web applications and APIs. Its minimalist design and extensible architecture make it an ideal choice for projects of all sizes, from small prototypes to large-scale applications. By understanding Flask's core principles and leveraging its features, developers can unlock the power of web development and create innovative solutions that drive the future of technology. Whether building dynamic web pages, RESTful APIs, or full-fledged web applications, Flask empowers developers to bring their ideas to life and shape the digital landscape.

Chapter 3

Getting Started with Flask - Your First Steps into the API Dojo

Setting Up Your Development Environment: Tools of the Trade

Setting up a robust development environment is crucial for efficient and productive software development. From code editors and version control systems to package managers and testing frameworks, developers rely on a variety of tools to streamline their workflow and enhance productivity. In this essay, we will explore the essential tools and techniques for setting up a development environment tailored for Flask API development. Through code examples and practical demonstrations, we will showcase the tools of the trade and provide guidance on configuring an efficient development environment.

1. Code Editor:

Choosing the right code editor is essential for comfortable and productive coding sessions. While there are numerous options available, some popular choices among developers include Visual Studio Code, Sublime Text, and Atom. These code editors offer features such as syntax highlighting, code completion, and integrated terminal, making them well-suited for Flask development.

2. Version Control System (VCS):

Version control systems allow developers to track changes to their codebase, collaborate with team members, and manage project history effectively. Git, a distributed version control system, is widely used in the software development industry. Platforms like GitHub, GitLab, and Bitbucket provide hosting services for Git repositories, enabling seamless collaboration and code sharing.

To initialize a Git repository for a Flask project, navigate to the project directory and run the following commands:

```bash
git init
git add .
git commit -m "Initial commit"
```

This initializes a new Git repository, stages all files in the directory for commit, and creates an initial commit with a descriptive message.

3. Package Manager:

Package managers simplify the process of installing and managing dependencies for a project. For Python projects, pip is the de facto standard package manager. With pip, developers can easily install Flask and other dependencies required for their project.

To install Flask using pip, run the following command in your terminal:

```bash
pip install Flask
```

This command installs the latest version of Flask from the Python Package Index (PyPI) and makes it available for use in your project.

4. Virtual Environment:

Virtual environments provide a sandboxed environment for isolating project dependencies and ensuring consistency across different projects. Virtualenv is a popular tool for creating virtual environments in Python projects.

To create a virtual environment for a Flask project, navigate to the project directory and run the following commands:

```bash
pip install virtualenv
virtualenv venv
```

This creates a new virtual environment named `venv` in the project directory. To activate the virtual environment, run:

- On Windows:

```bash
venv\Scripts\activate
```

- On macOS and Linux:

```bash
source venv/bin/activate
```

Once activated, the virtual environment isolates dependencies and ensures that packages installed in the environment do not affect other projects.

5. Flask CLI (Command-Line Interface):

Flask provides a built-in command-line interface (CLI) for performing common tasks such as running the development server, managing database migrations, and creating project scaffolding. The Flask CLI simplifies the development workflow and automates repetitive tasks, improving productivity.

To use the Flask CLI, install Flask in your virtual environment and run the following command to create a new Flask project:

```bash
flask init
```

This command generates the necessary files and directories for a Flask project, including the `app.py` file, which serves as the entry point for the application.

6. Testing Framework:

Testing is an integral part of software development, ensuring that code behaves as expected and remains robust in the face of changes. For Flask projects, pytest is a popular testing framework that provides a simple and flexible way to write and run tests.

To install pytest in your virtual environment, run the following command:

```bash
pip install pytest
```

You can then write test cases using pytest's simple and expressive syntax and run tests using the `pytest` command.

Setting up a development environment tailored for Flask API development requires careful consideration of tools and techniques that streamline the development workflow and enhance productivity. By choosing the right code editor, version control system, package manager, virtual environment, Flask CLI, and testing framework, developers can create a robust and efficient development environment that facilitates the creation of high-quality Flask applications and APIs. With the right tools at their disposal, developers can focus on building innovative solutions and pushing the boundaries of web development with Flask.

Creating Your First Flask Application: Hello, World (API Style)!

Embarking on the journey of Flask development is an exciting endeavor that opens the doors to creating powerful web applications and APIs. In this essay, we will guide you through the process of creating your first Flask application in the API style, where you will learn the fundamentals of Flask API development. By following along with code examples and practical demonstrations, you will gain a solid understanding of how to create a basic Flask API that responds with "Hello, World!".

Setting Up the Environment:

Before we dive into creating our Flask application, let's ensure that we have our development environment set up properly. Make sure you have Python installed on your system, along with pip for managing Python packages. Additionally, it's recommended to set up a virtual environment to isolate our project dependencies.

```bash
# Install virtualenv if you haven't already
pip install virtualenv

# Create a new virtual environment named 'flask-env'
```

```
virtualenv flask-env

# Activate the virtual environment
# On Windows:
flask-env\Scripts\activate
# On macOS and Linux:
source flask-env/bin/activate
```

Once the virtual environment is activated, we can proceed to install Flask using pip:

```bash
pip install Flask
```

Creating the Flask Application:

Now that our environment is set up, let's create our first Flask application. We'll start by creating a new Python file named `app.py` in our project directory.

```python
from flask import Flask

app = Flask(__name__)

@app.route('/')
```

```
def hello_world():
    return 'Hello, World!'

if __name__ == '__main__':
    app.run(debug=True)
```

In this code, we import the Flask class from the Flask module and create an instance of the Flask class named `app`. We then define a route `/` using the `@app.route()` decorator, which maps requests to the root URL to the `hello_world()` function. Inside the `hello_world()` function, we return the string "Hello, World!".

Running the Flask Application:

To run our Flask application, we need to execute the `app.py` file. Since we set the `debug` parameter to `True`, Flask will automatically reload the application when changes are detected.

```bash
python app.py
```

Once the application is running, you should see output similar to the following:

```
 * Running on http://127.0.0.1:5000/ (Press CTRL+C to quit)
```

Now, open a web browser and navigate to `http://127.0.0.1:5000/`. You should see the message "Hello, World!" displayed in the browser window. Congratulations! You've successfully created your first Flask application.

Enhancing the API:

While our "Hello, World!" API is a great starting point, let's enhance it by adding support for JSON responses and dynamic routes. We'll modify our `app.py` file to demonstrate these enhancements:

```python
from flask import Flask, jsonify

app = Flask(__name__)

@app.route('/')
def hello_world():
    return 'Hello, World!'
```

```
@app.route('/api/greet/<name>')
def greet_user(name):
    return jsonify({'message': f'Hello, {name}!'})

if __name__ == '__main__':
    app.run(debug=True)
```
```

In this updated version of our application, we've added a new route `/api/greet/<name>` that accepts a dynamic parameter `name`. The `greet_user()` function retrieves the `name` parameter from the URL and returns a JSON response containing a personalized greeting message.

**Testing the Enhanced API:**

To test our enhanced API, restart the Flask application by stopping it using `Ctrl+C` in the terminal and then running `python app.py` again. Once the application is running, open a web browser and navigate to `http://127.0.0.1:5000/api/greet/John` (replace "John" with your name). You should see a JSON response with the message "Hello, John!" displayed in the browser window.

Creating your first Flask application is an exciting milestone in your journey as a web developer. In this essay, we walked through the process of setting up a
```

development environment, creating a basic Flask application, and enhancing it with dynamic routes and JSON responses. Armed with this knowledge, you're well-equipped to explore further and build more complex Flask applications and APIs. Keep experimenting, learning, and building, and you'll soon be on your way to mastering Flask development. Happy coding!

Running and Testing Your Flask App: Debugging Like a Pro

Running and testing your Flask application are crucial steps in the development process to ensure your app behaves as expected and is free from errors. In this essay, we'll explore best practices for running and testing Flask apps, covering debugging techniques, testing methodologies, and tools to streamline the development workflow. By following along with code examples and practical demonstrations, you'll learn how to debug your Flask app like a pro and write effective tests to ensure its reliability and robustness.

Running Your Flask App:

Running your Flask app is the first step in the development process, allowing you to interact with the application and test its functionality. Flask provides a built-in development server that you can use to run your app locally during the development phase.

To run your Flask app, navigate to the directory containing your app's Python file (e.g., `app.py`) and execute the following command in your terminal:

```bash
python app.py
```

This command starts the Flask development server and serves your app on the default address `http://127.0.0.1:5000/`. You can now access your app in a web browser by navigating to this address.

Debugging Your Flask App:

Debugging is an essential skill for any developer, allowing you to identify and fix issues in your code efficiently. Flask provides built-in debugging tools that help you diagnose problems and trace the execution flow of your app.

One of the most useful debugging features in Flask is the built-in debugger, which provides detailed error messages and a traceback of the code execution when an exception occurs. To enable the debugger, set the `debug` parameter to `True` when creating the Flask app instance:

```python
from flask import Flask

app = Flask(__name__)

# Enable Flask debugger
app.debug = True

@app.route('/')
def hello_world():
    return 'Hello, Flask!'
```

With the debugger enabled, Flask will display detailed error messages and a stack trace in the browser window when an exception occurs during the execution of your app. This information is invaluable for identifying the cause of the error and debugging your code effectively.

Testing Your Flask App:

Testing is a critical aspect of software development, ensuring that your app behaves as expected and remains reliable under different conditions. Flask provides a variety of tools and frameworks for writing and running tests, allowing you to automate the testing process and catch bugs early in the development cycle.

One popular testing framework for Flask applications is pytest, which provides a simple and expressive syntax for writing tests and powerful features for test discovery and execution.

To get started with pytest, install it in your virtual environment using pip:

```bash
pip install pytest
```

Once pytest is installed, you can write test cases for your Flask app in separate Python files using the pytest framework. Let's write a simple test case to verify that our Flask app returns the correct response when accessing the root URL:

Create a new Python file named `test_app.py` in your project directory and add the following code:

```python
from app import app

import pytest
```

```python
@pytest.fixture
def client():
    app.config['TESTING'] = True
    with app.test_client() as client:
        yield client

def test_hello_world(client):
    response = client.get('/')
    assert response.status_code == 200
    assert b'Hello, Flask!' in response.data
```

In this test case, we define a fixture named `client` that creates a test client for our Flask app with testing mode enabled. We then write a test function named `test_hello_world` that sends a GET request to the root URL (`/`) and asserts that the response status code is 200 (OK) and that the response data contains the expected message "Hello, Flask!".

To run the test, execute the following command in your terminal:

```bash
pytest
```

Pytest will automatically discover and run all test files in your project directory, displaying the results in the terminal window. If the test passes, you'll see a green dot indicating success. If the test fails, pytest will provide detailed information about the failure, allowing you to identify and fix the issue.

Running and testing your Flask app are essential steps in the development process to ensure its functionality, reliability, and robustness. By leveraging Flask's built-in debugging tools and testing frameworks like pytest, you can diagnose issues, write effective tests, and catch bugs early in the development cycle. With the knowledge and techniques covered in this essay, you'll be well-equipped to debug your Flask app like a pro and write thorough tests to ensure its quality and stability. Happy coding!

Chapter 4

Crafting Powerful Endpoints - The Gates to Your API Kingdom

Demystifying Endpoints: The Entry Points for Data Flow

In the world of web development, endpoints serve as the entry points for data flow in APIs (Application Programming Interfaces). Understanding endpoints is crucial for building effective APIs that enable communication between clients and servers. In this essay, we will demystify endpoints, exploring their significance, structure, and implementation in Flask API development. Through code examples and practical demonstrations, we will elucidate the role of endpoints as the gateways for data exchange in web applications.

Understanding Endpoints:

Endpoints are specific URLs that are exposed by an API and represent resources or actions that clients can interact with. Each endpoint typically corresponds to a specific function or set of operations on the server side, allowing clients to retrieve, create, update, or delete resources as needed.

In the context of Flask API development, endpoints are defined using the `@app.route()` decorator, which associates URL patterns with corresponding Python functions (view functions). These view functions handle incoming requests to the specified endpoints and return appropriate responses based on the requested resource or action.

Let's delve into an example to illustrate the concept of endpoints in Flask:

```python
from flask import Flask

app = Flask(__name__)

# Define endpoint for the root URL

@app.route('/')

def index():

    return 'Welcome to the API homepage!'

# Define endpoint for retrieving user information

@app.route('/users/<username>')

def get_user(username):

    return f'Retrieving information for user: {username}'

# Define endpoint for creating a new user

@app.route('/users', methods=['POST'])

def create_user():
```

```
    # Logic to create a new user

    return 'User created successfully'
# Define endpoint for updating user information

@app.route('/users/<username>', methods=['PUT'])

def update_user(username):

    # Logic to update user information

    return f'Updating information for user: {username}'
# Define endpoint for deleting a user

@app.route('/users/<username>', methods=['DELETE'])

def delete_user(username):

    # Logic to delete user

    return f'Deleting user: {username}'
if __name__ == '__main__':

    app.run(debug=True)
```

In this Flask application, we define several endpoints to handle various operations related to user management:

- The root URL `/` serves as the homepage of the API.
- The `/users/<username>` endpoint allows clients to retrieve, update, or delete information for a specific user identified by their username.
- The `/users` endpoint supports the creation of new users via HTTP POST requests.

Each endpoint is associated with a specific URL pattern and HTTP method, allowing clients to interact with the API and perform CRUD (Create, Read, Update, Delete) operations on user resources.

<u>Implementing Endpoints in Flask:</u>

To implement endpoints in Flask, we use the `@app.route()` decorator to define routes and associate them with view functions. The decorator takes two main arguments: the URL pattern and the HTTP methods supported by the endpoint.

```python
@app.route('/endpoint', methods=['GET'])
def endpoint_function():
    # Logic to handle the endpoint
    return 'Response'
```

In the above example, we define an endpoint `/endpoint` that supports HTTP GET requests. When a client sends a GET request to this endpoint, the `endpoint_function()` is invoked, and the return value is sent back as the response.

Endpoints can also accept dynamic parameters in the URL, allowing for more flexible routing and resource identification. Dynamic parameters are specified using angle brackets (`<parameter_name>`), and their values are extracted from the URL and passed as arguments to the view function.

```python

@app.route('/users/<username>')

def get_user(username):

    # Logic to retrieve user information

    return f'Retrieving information for user: {username}'

```

In this example, the `/users/<username>` endpoint accepts a dynamic parameter `username`, allowing clients to retrieve information for a specific user by specifying their username in the URL.

Testing Endpoints:

Testing endpoints is an essential part of API development to ensure that they behave as expected and return the correct responses under different conditions. Flask provides tools and libraries for writing and executing tests for endpoints, allowing developers to automate the testing process and catch bugs early in the development cycle.

One popular testing framework for Flask applications is pytest, which provides a simple and expressive syntax for writing tests and powerful features for test discovery and execution.

Let's write a simple test case to verify the behavior of the `/users/<username>` endpoint in our Flask application:

```python
import pytest

from app import app

@pytest.fixture
def client():
    app.config['TESTING'] = True
    with app.test_client() as client:
        yield client

def test_get_user(client):
    response = client.get('/users/johndoe')
```

```
        assert response.status_code == 200

        assert b'Retrieving information for user: johndoe' in response.data

```

In this test case, we use pytest fixtures to create a test client for our Flask app with testing mode enabled. We then write a test function named `test_get_user` that sends a GET request to the `/users/johndoe` endpoint and asserts that the response status code is 200 (OK) and that the response data contains the expected message.

Endpoints serve as the entry points for data flow in APIs, allowing clients to interact with resources and perform operations on the server side. In this essay, we demystified endpoints in the context of Flask API development, exploring their significance, structure, and implementation. By leveraging Flask's routing system and testing frameworks like pytest, developers can create robust APIs with well-defined endpoints and ensure their reliability and functionality through comprehensive testing. With a solid understanding of endpoints

HTTP Methods Demystified: GET, POST, PUT, and DELETE Explained

HTTP (Hypertext Transfer Protocol) methods are the backbone of communication on the web. They define the actions that can be performed on a resource identified by a URL. In this guide, we'll delve into the most common HTTP methods: GET, POST, PUT, and DELETE, and explore how they are used in API development with Flask, a lightweight Python web framework.

Understanding HTTP Methods

1. GET Method

The GET method is used to request data from a specified resource. It retrieves data without altering it, making it a safe and idempotent operation. GET requests should only be used for retrieving data and should not have any side effects on the server.

Example:

```python
from flask import Flask, request

app = Flask(__name__)

@app.route('/books', methods=['GET'])
def get_books():
    # Retrieve books data
    # Return data as response
    return "List of books..."

if __name__ == '__main__':
    app.run(debug=True)
```

```

## 2. POST Method

The POST method is used to submit data to be processed to a specified resource. It is commonly used for creating new resources on the server. Unlike GET, POST requests may have side effects on the server, such as adding or modifying data.

**Example**:

```python

@app.route('/books', methods=['POST'])

def create_book():

   # Extract data from request

   # Process data (e.g., save to database)

   return "Book created successfully"

```

3. PUT Method

The PUT method is used to update data on the server. It replaces the current representation of the target resource with the request payload. PUT requests are idempotent, meaning that multiple identical requests should have the same effect as a single request.
```

Example:

```python
@app.route('/books/<int:id>', methods=['PUT'])
def update_book(id):
    # Extract data from request
    # Update book with specified ID
    return "Book updated successfully"
```

4. DELETE Method

The DELETE method is used to remove a resource from the server. It is used to delete the resource identified by the URL. Like PUT requests, DELETE requests are idempotent.

Example:

```python
@app.route('/books/<int:id>', methods=['DELETE'])
def delete_book(id):
    # Delete book with specified ID
```

```
    return "Book deleted successfully"
```

Using HTTP Methods in Flask

Setting Up Flask Application

Before we can start using HTTP methods in Flask, we need to set up a Flask application. Install Flask if you haven't already:

```bash
pip install Flask
```

Now, let's create a basic Flask application:

```python
from flask import Flask

app = Flask(__name__)

if __name__ == '__main__':
    app.run(debug=True)
```

Creating Routes

Now that we have our Flask application set up, let's create routes for handling different HTTP methods.

GET Request

```python
@app.route('/books', methods=['GET'])
def get_books():
    # Retrieve books data
    # Return data as response
    return "List of books..."
```

POST Request

```python
@app.route('/books', methods=['POST'])
def create_book():
    # Extract data from request
    # Process data (e.g., save to database)
    return "Book created successfully"
```

PUT Request

```python
@app.route('/books/<int:id>', methods=['PUT'])
def update_book(id):
    # Extract data from request
    # Update book with specified ID
    return "Book updated successfully"
```

DELETE Request

```python
@app.route('/books/<int:id>', methods=['DELETE'])
def delete_book(id):
    # Delete book with specified ID
    return "Book deleted successfully"
```

Testing HTTP Methods

To test our Flask application and the HTTP methods, we can use tools like cURL or Postman.

cURL Example

GET Request

```bash
curl -X GET http://localhost:5000/books
```

POST Request

```bash
curl -X POST http://localhost:5000/books -d "title=New Book&author=John Doe"
```

PUT Request

```bash
curl -X PUT http://localhost:5000/books/1 -d "title=Updated Book&author=Jane Doe"
```

DELETE Request

```bash
curl -X DELETE http://localhost:5000/books/1
```

```

HTTP methods are essential for building RESTful APIs. Understanding the differences between GET, POST, PUT, and DELETE, and how to use them effectively in Flask, is crucial for developing robust web applications. By following the examples in this guide, you can start building powerful APIs with Flask and handle various CRUD operations seamlessly.

## Building Dynamic Endpoints with Flask Routing: URL Magic

Flask, a micro web framework for Python, provides powerful routing capabilities that allow developers to build dynamic endpoints for their applications. In this guide, we'll explore Flask's URL routing and learn how to create dynamic endpoints that respond to different URL patterns.

### Understanding Flask Routing

Routing in Flask refers to the process of mapping URLs to view functions. Each route definition consists of a URL pattern and a corresponding view function. When a request matches a defined URL pattern, Flask invokes the associated view function to handle the request.

### Basic Routing Example

Let's start with a basic example of routing in Flask:

```python

```
from flask import Flask

app = Flask(__name__)

@app.route('/')

def index():

    return 'Welcome to the homepage'

@app.route('/about')

def about():

    return 'About Us'

if __name__ == '__main__':

    app.run(debug=True)
```
```

In this example, we have defined two routes: `'/'` and `'/about'`. The `index()` function handles requests to the root URL (`'/'`), while the `about()` function handles requests to `'/about'`.

Dynamic Endpoints with Variable Rules

Flask allows us to create dynamic endpoints by using variable rules in route definitions. Variable rules are placeholders within the URL pattern that capture parts of the URL and pass them as arguments to the view function.
```

Basic Variable Rules Example

```python
from flask import Flask

app = Flask(__name__)

@app.route('/user/<username>')
def profile(username):
    return f'User Profile: {username}'

if __name__ == '__main__':
    app.run(debug=True)
```

In this example, the `/user/<username>` route pattern contains a variable rule `<username>`, which captures any value in the URL segment after `/user/`. The captured value is then passed as an argument to the `profile()` function.

Variable Rules with Data Types

Flask allows us to specify the data type of variables in variable rules. We can define variable rules with specific data types such as `int`, `float`, and `path`.

```python
```

```python
from flask import Flask

app = Flask(__name__)

@app.route('/post/<int:post_id>')

def show_post(post_id):

    return f'Post ID: {post_id}'

if __name__ == '__main__':

    app.run(debug=True)
```

In this example, the `<int:post_id>` variable rule specifies that the `post_id` parameter must be an integer. If a non-integer value is provided in the URL, Flask will return a 404 Not Found error.

Building Dynamic Endpoints

Now that we understand how variable rules work in Flask routing, let's explore how we can build dynamic endpoints for our applications.

Example: Retrieving User Information

```python
from flask import Flask, jsonify

app = Flask(__name__)
```

```python
# Dummy user data
users = {
    1: {'name': 'John', 'age': 30},
    2: {'name': 'Jane', 'age': 25}
}
@app.route('/user/<int:user_id>')
def get_user(user_id):
    user = users.get(user_id)
    if user:
        return jsonify(user)
    else:
        return jsonify({'error': 'User not found'}), 404
if __name__ == '__main__':
    app.run(debug=True)
```
```

In this example, we define a route `'/user/<int:user_id>'` to retrieve user information based on the `user_id` provided in the URL. The `get_user()` function retrieves
```

the user data from a dictionary based on the `user_id` and returns it as JSON.

Advanced Dynamic Endpoints

Flask's routing capabilities extend beyond simple variable rules. We can create more complex dynamic endpoints using regular expressions and custom converters.

Example: Custom Converter for UUIDs

```python
from flask import Flask

from werkzeug.routing import BaseConverter

app = Flask(__name__)

class UUIDConverter(BaseConverter):
    def to_python(self, value):
        # Validate UUID format
        return value

    def to_url(self, value):
        return str(value)

app.url_map.converters['uuid'] = UUIDConverter
```

```
@app.route('/document/<uuid:doc_id>')
def get_document(doc_id):
    # Retrieve document based on UUID
    return f'Document ID: {doc_id}'

if __name__ == '__main__':
    app.run(debug=True)
```

In this example, we define a custom converter `UUIDConverter` to handle UUIDs in URL paths. The converter validates the UUID format and passes it as an argument to the `get_document()` function.

Flask's flexible routing system enables developers to create dynamic endpoints for their applications. By leveraging variable rules, data type specifications, regular expressions, and custom converters, Flask allows for the creation of powerful and expressive APIs. Understanding Flask's URL routing capabilities is essential for building scalable and maintainable web applications.

Chapter 5

Data Wrangling with Flask - Taming the Data Flow

Understanding Data Serialization: Making Data Travel-Ready

Serialization is the process of converting complex data structures or objects into a format that can be easily transmitted over a network or stored in a file. In the context of web development, data serialization is crucial for exchanging data between clients and servers in a format that both parties can understand. In this guide, we'll explore the importance of data serialization and how it's implemented in Flask, a lightweight Python web framework.

Why Data Serialization Matters

When building web applications, data is often exchanged between clients and servers in the form of JSON (JavaScript Object Notation) or XML (eXtensible Markup Language). These formats are commonly used because they are human-readable and widely supported across different programming languages and platforms.

Data serialization allows developers to:

- Transmit complex data structures over HTTP.
- Store data in databases or files.

- Maintain consistency in data representation across different systems.

Serialization Formats

The two most common serialization formats used in web development are JSON and XML.

JSON (JavaScript Object Notation)

JSON is a lightweight data interchange format that is easy for humans to read and write and easy for machines to parse and generate. It is based on a subset of the JavaScript programming language.

Example of JSON data:

```json
{
  "name": "John Doe",
  "age": 30,
  "email": "john@example.com"
}
```

XML (eXtensible Markup Language)

XML is a markup language that defines a set of rules for encoding documents in a format that is both human-readable and machine-readable.

Example of XML data:

```xml
<person>
  <name>John Doe</name>
  <age>30</age>
  <email>john@example.com</email>
</person>
```

Serialization in Flask

Flask provides built-in support for data serialization through its `jsonify()` function, which converts Python objects into JSON-formatted responses.

Example: Serializing Data with Flask

```python
from flask import Flask, jsonify

app = Flask(__name__)
```

```
@app.route('/user')
def get_user():
    user = {
        'name': 'John Doe',
        'age': 30,
        'email': 'john@example.com'
    }
    return jsonify(user)

if __name__ == '__main__':
    app.run(debug=True)
```

In this example, the `get_user()` function returns a dictionary representing user data. Flask's `jsonify()` function is used to serialize the data into JSON format before sending it as a response to the client.

Deserialization

Deserialization is the process of converting serialized data back into its original data structure or object. In the context of web development, deserialization is commonly used to process incoming data from client requests.

Flask provides support for deserializing JSON data using the `request.json` attribute, which contains the parsed JSON data from the request body.

Example: Deserializing Data with Flask

```python
from flask import Flask, request, jsonify

app = Flask(__name__)

@app.route('/user', methods=['POST'])

def create_user():

    data = request.json

    # Process incoming JSON data

    return jsonify(data), 201

if __name__ == '__main__':

    app.run(debug=True)
```

In this example, the `create_user()` function retrieves the JSON data from the request body using `request.json` and processes it accordingly.

Choosing the Right Serialization Format

When deciding on a serialization format for your application, consider the following factors:

- **Compatibility**: Ensure that the chosen format is supported by both clients and servers.
- **Efficiency**: Choose a format that minimizes data size and processing overhead.
- **Readability**: Prioritize human-readable formats for ease of debugging and maintenance.
- **Security**: Be mindful of security vulnerabilities such as JSON injection and XML external entity (XXE) attacks.

Data serialization is a fundamental concept in web development, enabling the exchange of data between clients and servers in a format that is both efficient and easy to interpret. By understanding the importance of data serialization and leveraging Flask's built-in support for JSON serialization, developers can build robust and scalable web applications that effectively communicate with clients and other backend systems.

Working with JSON: The Universal Language of APIs

JSON (JavaScript Object Notation) has become the de facto standard for data interchange on the web. It's lightweight, human-readable, and easy to parse, making it an ideal format for APIs to communicate data between clients and servers. In this guide, we'll explore the importance of JSON in API development and how to work with JSON data in Flask, a popular Python web framework.

Understanding JSON

JSON is a text-based data interchange format that is based on a subset of the JavaScript programming language. It consists of key-value pairs and supports nested structures such as arrays and objects. JSON is commonly used for transmitting data between a server and a client in web applications.

Example of JSON Data

```json
{
  "name": "John Doe",
  "age": 30,
  "email": "john@example.com",
  "address": {
    "city": "New York",
    "country": "USA"
  },
  "tags": ["developer", "python", "flask"]
```

}
```

## JSON in API Development

JSON plays a crucial role in API development as it provides a standardized format for exchanging data between different systems. APIs typically use JSON as the primary format for request and response payloads, allowing clients to consume data from the server and vice versa.

## Benefits of Using JSON in APIs

- **Interoperability**: JSON is supported by most programming languages and platforms, making it easy to integrate with various systems.
- **Human-Readable:** JSON is easy for humans to read and write, facilitating debugging and troubleshooting.
- **Compactness**: JSON data is lightweight and concise, minimizing network bandwidth usage and improving performance.
- **Flexibility**: JSON supports complex data structures, including nested objects and arrays, allowing for rich data representations.

## Working with JSON in Flask

Flask provides built-in support for JSON serialization and deserialization, making it easy to work with JSON data in Flask-based APIs.
```

Serializing Data to JSON

Flask's `jsonify()` function is used to serialize Python objects into JSON-formatted responses. It takes a dictionary or a list of dictionaries as input and returns a JSON response.

```python
from flask import Flask, jsonify

app = Flask(__name__)

@app.route('/user')
def get_user():
    user = {
        "name": "John Doe",
        "age": 30,
        "email": "john@example.com"
    }
    return jsonify(user)

if __name__ == '__main__':
    app.run(debug=True)
```

In this example, the `get_user()` function returns user data as a dictionary, which is then serialized into JSON format using `jsonify()` before being sent as a response to the client.

Deserializing JSON Data

Flask's `request.json` attribute allows us to access JSON data sent in the body of a request. It automatically parses the JSON data into a Python dictionary, making it easy to work with in our Flask routes.

```python
from flask import Flask, request, jsonify

app = Flask(__name__)

@app.route('/user', methods=['POST'])
def create_user():
    data = request.json
    # Process JSON data
    return jsonify(data), 201

if __name__ == '__main__':
    app.run(debug=True)
```

In this example, the `create_user()` function retrieves JSON data from the request body using `request.json` and processes it accordingly.

Error Handling with JSON

Flask allows us to return JSON-formatted error responses using the `jsonify()` function. This ensures consistency in the API's response format and makes it easier for clients to handle errors programmatically.

```python
from flask import Flask, jsonify

app = Flask(__name__)

@app.route('/user/<int:user_id>')
def get_user(user_id):
    user = find_user_by_id(user_id)
    if user:
        return jsonify(user)
    else:
        return jsonify({'error': 'User not found'}), 404

if __name__ == '__main__':
    app.run(debug=True)
```

```

In this example, if the user is not found, the function returns a JSON-formatted error response with a status code of 404 (Not Found).

JSON is the universal language of APIs, serving as a standardized format for data interchange in web development. By leveraging Flask's built-in support for JSON serialization and deserialization, developers can easily work with JSON data in their Flask-based APIs. Understanding how to serialize data to JSON responses, deserialize JSON data from requests, and handle errors with JSON-formatted responses is essential for building robust and scalable web APIs with Flask.

## Handling User Input with Flask Request Objects: Extracting Data with Ease

In web development, handling user input is a fundamental aspect of building interactive applications. Flask, a lightweight Python web framework, provides powerful tools for extracting and processing user input through request objects. In this guide, we'll explore how to handle user input with Flask request objects, covering various methods for extracting data from requests.

### Understanding Flask Request Objects

Flask request objects provide access to incoming HTTP request data such as form data, query parameters, JSON payloads, and more. These objects contain attributes and
```

methods for accessing different parts of the request data, making it easy to extract and process user input.

Types of Request Data

Flask request objects support the following types of request data:

- **Form Data:** Data submitted via HTML forms using the POST method.
- **Query Parameters:** Key-value pairs included in the URL query string.
- **JSON Payloads:** Data sent in the body of a request in JSON format.
- **Cookies**: HTTP cookies sent by the client.

Extracting Form Data

Form data is commonly used to collect user input in web applications. Flask provides the `request.form` attribute to access form data submitted via HTML forms.

Example: Handling Form Data

```python
from flask import Flask, request

app = Flask(__name__)

@app.route('/submit', methods=['POST'])

def submit_form():
```

```python
    name = request.form.get('name')
    email = request.form.get('email')
    # Process form data
    return f'Name: {name}, Email: {email}'

if __name__ == '__main__':
    app.run(debug=True)
```

In this example, the `submit_form()` function extracts form data using the `request.form.get()` method and processes it accordingly.

Extracting Query Parameters

Query parameters are key-value pairs included in the URL query string. Flask provides the `request.args` attribute to access query parameters.

Example: Handling Query Parameters

```python
from flask import Flask, request

app = Flask(__name__)

@app.route('/search')
```

```python
def search():
    query = request.args.get('q')
    # Perform search based on query parameter
    return f'Search query: {query}'

if __name__ == '__main__':
    app.run(debug=True)
```

In this example, the `search()` function extracts the `q` query parameter using the `request.args.get()` method and performs a search operation based on the provided query.

Extracting JSON Payloads

JSON payloads are commonly used in API development for sending data in the body of a request. Flask provides the `request.json` attribute to access JSON data sent in the request body.

Example: Handling JSON Payloads

```python
from flask import Flask, request

app = Flask(__name__)
```

```python
@app.route('/submit', methods=['POST'])
def submit_json():
    data = request.json
    name = data.get('name')
    email = data.get('email')
    # Process JSON data
    return f'Name: {name}, Email: {email}'

if __name__ == '__main__':
    app.run(debug=True)
```

In this example, the `submit_json()` function extracts JSON data from the request body using the `request.json` attribute and processes it accordingly.

Accessing Cookies

Cookies are small pieces of data sent by the server and stored on the client's browser. Flask provides the `request.cookies` attribute to access cookies sent by the client.

Example: Accessing Cookies

```python
```

```
from flask import Flask, request

app = Flask(__name__)

@app.route('/')

def index():

    username = request.cookies.get('username')

    # Display personalized content based on cookie

    return f'Welcome back, {username}'

if __name__ == '__main__':

    app.run(debug=True)
```

In this example, the `index()` function retrieves the `username` cookie using the `request.cookies.get()` method and displays personalized content based on the cookie value.

File Uploads

Flask also supports file uploads through request objects. The `request.files` attribute allows you to access files uploaded via HTML forms with the enctype set to `multipart/form-data`.

Example: Handling File Uploads

```python
from flask import Flask, request

app = Flask(__name__)

@app.route('/upload', methods=['POST'])
def upload_file():
    file = request.files['file']
    # Process uploaded file
    return f'File uploaded: {file.filename}'

if __name__ == '__main__':
    app.run(debug=True)
```

In this example, the `upload_file()` function retrieves the uploaded file using the `request.files` attribute and processes it accordingly.

Flask request objects provide a convenient and flexible way to handle user input in web applications. By leveraging attributes and methods such as `request.form`, `request.args`, `request.json`, and `request.cookies`, developers can easily extract and process form data, query parameters, JSON payloads, cookies, and file uploads. Understanding how to work with Flask request objects is essential for building interactive and data-driven web applications with Flask.

Sending Responses Back: Returning Data to the User

In web development, sending responses back to clients is a crucial aspect of building APIs and web applications. Flask, a lightweight Python web framework, provides various methods for returning data to users based on their requests. In this guide, we'll explore how to send responses back to users in Flask, covering different types of responses and status codes.

Sending Basic Responses

Flask allows developers to return basic text or HTML responses using simple return statements within route functions.

Example: Sending Text Response

```python
from flask import Flask

app = Flask(__name__)

@app.route('/')
def index():
    return 'Hello, World!'
```

```
if __name__ == '__main__':
    app.run(debug=True)
```

In this example, the `index()` function returns a simple text response of "Hello, World!" when the root URL is accessed.

Example: Sending HTML Response

```python
from flask import Flask

app = Flask(__name__)

@app.route('/')
def index():
    return '<h1>Hello, World!</h1>'

if __name__ == '__main__':
    app.run(debug=True)
```

In this example, the `index()` function returns an HTML response with a heading element containing the text "Hello, World!".

Returning JSON Responses

JSON (JavaScript Object Notation) is a popular data interchange format used in web development. Flask provides a convenient way to return JSON responses using the `jsonify()` function.

Example: Returning JSON Response

```python
from flask import Flask, jsonify

app = Flask(__name__)

@app.route('/user')
def get_user():
    user = {
        'name': 'John Doe',
        'age': 30,
        'email': 'john@example.com'
    }
    return jsonify(user)

if __name__ == '__main__':
    app.run(debug=True)
```

```

In this example, the `get_user()` function returns a JSON response containing user data.

**Setting Status Codes**

HTTP status codes indicate the success or failure of a request. Flask allows developers to set status codes for responses using the `status` parameter or by specifying the status code directly.

**Example: Setting Status Code**

```python
from flask import Flask, jsonify

app = Flask(__name__)

@app.route('/user')
def get_user():
    user = {
        'name': 'John Doe',
        'age': 30,
        'email': 'john@example.com'
    }

```
        return jsonify(user), 200

if __name__ == '__main__':

    app.run(debug=True)
```

In this example, the `get_user()` function returns a JSON response with a status code of 200 (OK).

Handling Errors

Flask provides mechanisms for handling errors and returning appropriate error responses to clients.

Example: Handling Not Found Error

```python
from flask import Flask, jsonify

app = Flask(__name__)

@app.route('/user/<int:user_id>')
def get_user(user_id):
    if user_id == 1:
        user = {
            'name': 'John Doe',
```

```
        'age': 30,
        'email': 'john@example.com'
    }
    return jsonify(user)
  else:
    return jsonify({'error': 'User not found'}), 404
if __name__ == '__main__':
  app.run(debug=True)
```

In this example, the `get_user()` function returns a JSON response with a status code of 404 (Not Found) if the requested user is not found.

Redirecting Responses

Flask allows developers to redirect users to different URLs using the `redirect()` function.

Example: Redirecting Users

```python
from flask import Flask, redirect, url_for

app = Flask(__name__)
```

```python
@app.route('/')
def index():
    return redirect(url_for('login'))

@app.route('/login')
def login():
    return 'Login Page'

if __name__ == '__main__':
    app.run(debug=True)
```

In this example, accessing the root URL (``/``) will redirect users to the login page (``/login``) using the `redirect()` function.

Streaming Responses

Flask supports streaming responses, allowing developers to send large amounts of data in chunks.

Example: Streaming Response

```python
from flask import Flask, Response

app = Flask(__name__)
```

```python
@app.route('/stream')
def stream_data():
    def generate():
        for i in range(10):
            yield f'Data Chunk {i}\n'
    return Response(generate(), mimetype='text/plain')

if __name__ == '__main__':
    app.run(debug=True)
```

In this example, the `stream_data()` function returns a streaming response containing 10 data chunks.

Custom Response Objects

Flask allows developers to create custom response objects using the `make_response()` function.

Example: Custom Response

```python
from flask import Flask, make_response

app = Flask(__name__)
```

```
@app.route('/')
def index():
    response = make_response('Hello, World!')
    response.headers['Custom-Header'] = 'Custom Value'
    return response

if __name__ == '__main__':
    app.run(debug=True)
```

In this example, the `index()` function creates a custom response object with a custom header.

Sending responses back to users is a fundamental aspect of web development, and Flask provides various methods for returning data to clients based on their requests. Whether returning basic text or HTML responses, JSON responses, setting status codes, handling errors, redirecting users, streaming responses, or creating custom response objects, Flask offers a range of options for sending responses back to users. Understanding how to use these features effectively is essential for building robust and interactive web applications with Flask.

Chapter 6

Error Handling and Validation - Building a Robust API Fortress

The Inevitable: Handling Errors Gracefully in Your API

Handling errors gracefully is a critical aspect of building reliable and user-friendly APIs. Errors can occur for various reasons, such as invalid input, server-side issues, or authentication failures. Flask, a lightweight Python web framework, provides robust mechanisms for handling errors and returning informative error responses to clients. In this guide, we'll explore how to handle errors gracefully in your Flask API, covering various types of errors and best practices for error handling.

Understanding Error Handling in Flask

Flask provides built-in support for handling errors through error handlers, which are functions that execute when specific error conditions occur. These error handlers allow developers to define custom behavior for different types of errors, ensuring that clients receive appropriate error responses.

Types of Errors

Common types of errors in API development include:

- **Client Errors:** Errors caused by invalid or malformed client requests (e.g. 400 Bad Request).
- **Server Errors:** Errors caused by server-side issues or unexpected failures (e.g., 500 Internal Server Error).
- **Authentication Errors:** Errors related to authentication and authorization failures (e.g., 401 Unauthorized, 403 Forbidden).
- **Not Found Errors:** Errors indicating that the requested resource does not exist (e.g., 404 Not Found).

Handling Client Errors

Client errors typically occur due to invalid input or incorrect usage of the API. Flask provides the `abort()` function to raise HTTP exceptions for different types of client errors.

Example: Handling 400 Bad Request Error

```python
from flask import Flask, abort, request

app = Flask(__name__)

@app.route('/user', methods=['POST'])
def create_user():
    data = request.json
    if not data or 'name' not in data:
```

```
        abort(400, 'Name is required')

    # Process user creation

    return 'User created successfully'

if __name__ == '__main__':

    app.run(debug=True)
```

In this example, the `create_user()` function checks if the request contains JSON data and if the 'name' field is present. If not, it aborts the request with a 400 Bad Request error and a custom error message.

Handling Server Errors

Server errors occur due to unexpected failures or issues on the server-side. Flask allows developers to define error handlers for server errors using the `@app.errorhandler()` decorator.

Example: Handling 500 Internal Server Error

```python
from flask import Flask, jsonify

app = Flask(__name__)

@app.route('/error')
```

```
def trigger_error():
    # Simulate server-side error
    raise Exception('Internal Server Error')

@app.errorhandler(500)
def internal_server_error(error):
    return jsonify({'error': 'Internal Server Error'}), 500

if __name__ == '__main__':
    app.run(debug=True)
```

In this example, accessing the `/error` route triggers a server-side error, which is caught by the `internal_server_error()` error handler and returns a JSON response with a 500 Internal Server Error status code.

Handling Authentication Errors

Authentication errors occur when clients attempt to access protected resources without proper authentication credentials. Flask provides mechanisms for handling authentication errors and returning appropriate error responses.

Example: Handling 401 Unauthorized Error

```python
from flask import Flask, jsonify, request, abort
app = Flask(__name__)
def authenticate(username, password):
    # Dummy authentication logic
    if username == 'admin' and password == 'password':
        return True
    else:
        return False
@app.route('/protected')
def protected_resource():
    auth_header = request.headers.get('Authorization')
    if not auth_header:
        abort(401, 'Authorization header is missing')
    token = auth_header.split()[1]
    if not authenticate_token(token):
        abort(401, 'Invalid token')
```

```
    # Process protected resource

    return 'Protected resource accessed successfully'

@app.errorhandler(401)

def unauthorized(error):

    return jsonify({'error': 'Unauthorized'}), 401

if __name__ == '__main__':

    app.run(debug=True)
```

In this example, the `protected_resource()` function checks for the presence of the Authorization header and verifies the authentication token. If authentication fails, it aborts the request with a 401 Unauthorized error, which is caught by the `unauthorized()` error handler and returns a JSON response with an appropriate error message.

Handling Not Found Errors

Not Found errors occur when clients attempt to access resources that do not exist. Flask provides mechanisms for handling Not Found errors and returning informative error responses.

Example: Handling 404 Not Found Error

```python
```

```python
from flask import Flask, jsonify

app = Flask(__name__)

@app.route('/user/<int:user_id>')

def get_user(user_id):
    # Retrieve user from database
    user = find_user_by_id(user_id)
    if not user:
        return jsonify({'error': 'User not found'}), 404
    return jsonify(user)

if __name__ == '__main__':
    app.run(debug=True)
```

In this example, the `get_user()` function attempts to retrieve a user from the database based on the provided user ID. If the user does not exist, it returns a JSON response with a 404 Not Found error.

Handling errors gracefully is essential for building reliable and user-friendly APIs. Flask provides robust mechanisms for handling various types of errors, including client errors, server errors, authentication errors, and Not Found errors. By leveraging error handlers and appropriate status codes, developers can ensure that clients receive informative error responses, enhancing the overall user experience of their APIs. Understanding how to handle errors gracefully is a critical skill for building resilient and scalable APIs with Flask.

Crafting Informative Error Messages: User-Friendly Troubleshooting

In API development, providing informative error messages is essential for enhancing the user experience and facilitating troubleshooting. When errors occur, clear and descriptive messages help users understand what went wrong and how to resolve the issue. Flask, a lightweight Python web framework, offers powerful tools for crafting informative error messages and returning them to clients. In this guide, we'll explore how to craft informative error messages in your Flask API, covering best practices and examples.

Importance of Informative Error Messages

Informative error messages serve several important purposes in API development:

1. Enhanced User Experience: Clear error messages help users understand why their requests failed and what actions they need to take to resolve the issue.

2. Troubleshooting: Informative error messages assist developers in identifying and debugging issues, leading to quicker resolution of problems.

3. Security: Providing detailed error messages without revealing sensitive information helps prevent potential security vulnerabilities.

Best Practices for Crafting Error Messages

When crafting error messages for your Flask API, consider the following best practices:

1. Be Specific: Provide detailed information about the nature of the error, including any relevant error codes or identifiers.

2. Be Clear and Concise: Keep error messages simple and easy to understand, avoiding technical jargon whenever possible.

3. Offer Guidance: Provide actionable steps or suggestions for users to resolve the issue, if applicable.

4. Protect Sensitive Information: Avoid exposing sensitive data or internal system details in error messages to prevent potential security risks.

5. Consistency: Maintain consistency in error message format and structure across different parts of your API.

Crafting Informative Error Messages in Flask

Flask provides various mechanisms for crafting and returning informative error messages to clients, including error handlers, custom exceptions, and response formatting.

Error Handlers

Flask error handlers allow developers to define custom behavior for different types of errors. By implementing error handlers, you can catch specific types of errors and return informative responses to clients.

Example: Custom Error Handler

```python
from flask import Flask, jsonify

app = Flask(__name__)

@app.route('/error')
def trigger_error():
    # Simulate server-side error
    raise Exception('Internal Server Error')

@app.errorhandler(Exception)
def handle_error(error):
    response = jsonify({'error': 'An unexpected error occurred'})
    response.status_code = 500
    return response
```

```python
if __name__ == '__main__':
    app.run(debug=True)
```

In this example, the `handle_error()` error handler catches any unexpected errors that occur in the application and returns a JSON response with a 500 Internal Server Error status code and a generic error message.

Custom Exceptions

Flask allows developers to define custom exceptions to represent specific error conditions in their APIs. Custom exceptions can encapsulate detailed information about the error and provide context for clients.

Example: Custom Exception

```python
from flask import Flask, jsonify

app = Flask(__name__)

class CustomException(Exception):
    def __init__(self, message, status_code=500):
        self.message = message
        self.status_code = status_code
```

```
@app.route('/user/<int:user_id>')
def get_user(user_id):
    user = find_user_by_id(user_id)
    if not user:
        raise CustomException('User not found', status_code=404)
    return jsonify(user)

@app.errorhandler(CustomException)
def handle_custom_exception(error):
    response = jsonify({'error': error.message})
    response.status_code = error.status_code
    return response

if __name__ == '__main__':
    app.run(debug=True)
```

In this example, the `CustomException` class represents a custom exception for handling the scenario where a requested user does not exist. The `handle_custom_exception()` error handler catches instances of this custom exception and returns a JSON response with a 404 Not Found status code and a specific error message.

Response Formatting

Flask provides flexibility in formatting error responses to meet the specific requirements of your API. You can customize the structure and content of error responses to include additional information or metadata as needed.

Example: Custom Error Response Format

```python
from flask import Flask, jsonify

app = Flask(__name__)

@app.route('/error')
def trigger_error():
    # Simulate server-side error
    raise Exception('Internal Server Error')

@app.errorhandler(Exception)
def handle_error(error):
    response = jsonify({
        'error': {
```

```
        'message': 'An unexpected error occurred',
        'code': 500
    }
    response.status_code = 500
    return response

if __name__ == '__main__':
    app.run(debug=True)
```

In this example, the `handle_error()` error handler formats the error response with a nested dictionary structure containing the error message and code. This custom format provides additional context about the error to clients.

Crafting informative error messages is essential for building user-friendly and reliable APIs. In Flask, you can leverage error handlers, custom exceptions, and response formatting to provide clear and descriptive error messages to clients. By following best practices and considering the needs of your users, you can enhance the user experience and streamline troubleshooting in your Flask API. Effective error message handling is a key aspect of building high-quality APIs that meet the expectations of your users.

Data Validation: Safeguarding Your API from Bad Data

Data validation is a crucial aspect of API development, ensuring that the data received from clients meets the expected criteria and quality standards. Validating data helps safeguard your API from potential security vulnerabilities, data corruption, and inconsistencies. Flask, a lightweight Python web framework, provides various tools and techniques for implementing data validation in your API. In this guide, we'll explore the importance of data validation and how to implement it effectively in Flask-based APIs.

Why Data Validation Matters

Data validation serves several important purposes in API development:

1. Security: Validating data helps prevent security vulnerabilities such as SQL injection, cross-site scripting (XSS), and injection attacks.

2. Data Integrity: Ensuring that data meets specified constraints and formats helps maintain data integrity and consistency within the system.

3. User Experience: Providing feedback to users about invalid data helps improve the user experience by guiding them to provide correct input.

Common Data Validation Techniques

There are several techniques for validating data in APIs, including:

1. Type Checking: Verifying that data types match the expected types (e.g., strings, integers, booleans).

2. Format Validation: Ensuring that data adheres to specified formats (e.g., email addresses, phone numbers, dates).

3. Length and Range Validation: Checking the length or range of numeric values or strings.

4. Presence Validation: Verifying that required fields are present and not empty.

5. Custom Validation: Implementing custom validation logic for complex data validation requirements.

Implementing Data Validation in Flask

Flask provides various mechanisms for implementing data validation in your API, including request validation, form validation, and custom validation logic.

Request Validation

Flask allows developers to access request data and perform validation directly within route functions using Flask's request object.

Example: Request Validation

```python
```

```
from flask import Flask, request, jsonify

app = Flask(__name__)

@app.route('/user', methods=['POST'])

def create_user():

    data = request.json

    if not data.get('name'):

        return jsonify({'error': 'Name is required'}), 400

    # Validate other fields...

    return jsonify({'message': 'User created successfully'})

if __name__ == '__main__':

    app.run(debug=True)
```

In this example, the `create_user()` function validates the presence of the 'name' field in the JSON request data. If the field is missing, it returns a JSON response with a 400 Bad Request error.

Form Validation

Flask-WTF, an extension for Flask, provides support for form validation using WTForms, a flexible form validation and rendering library for Python.

Example: Form Validation with Flask-WTF

```python
from flask import Flask, render_template
from flask_wtf import FlaskForm
from wtforms import StringField, SubmitField
from wtforms.validators import DataRequired

app = Flask(__name__)
app.config['SECRET_KEY'] = 'your_secret_key'

class UserForm(FlaskForm):
    name = StringField('Name', validators=[DataRequired()])
    email = StringField('Email', validators=[DataRequired()])
    submit = SubmitField('Submit')

@app.route('/user', methods=['GET', 'POST'])
def create_user():
    form = UserForm()
    if form.validate_on_submit():
```

```
# Process form data

return 'User created successfully'

return render_template('user_form.html', form=form)

if __name__ == '__main__':
    app.run(debug=True)
```

In this example, the `UserForm` class defines form fields with validators, such as `DataRequired()` for ensuring that fields are not empty. The `create_user()` function validates the form data upon submission and processes it if validation passes.

Custom Validation Logic

Flask allows developers to implement custom validation logic for complex data validation requirements using Python code within route functions.

Example: Custom Validation Logic

```python
from flask import Flask, request, jsonify

app = Flask(__name__)

def validate_email(email):
```

```
    # Custom email validation logic
    if '@' not in email:
        return False
    return True

@app.route('/user', methods=['POST'])
def create_user():
    data = request.json
    if not data.get('email') or not validate_email(data.get('email')):
        return jsonify({'error': 'Invalid email address'}), 400
    # Process other fields...
    return jsonify({'message': 'User created successfully'})

if __name__ == '__main__':
    app.run(debug=True)
```

In this example, the `validate_email()` function implements custom email validation logic, checking for the presence of the '@' symbol. The `create_user()` function uses this custom validation logic to validate the email address provided in the request data.

Data validation is essential for safeguarding your API from bad data and ensuring the integrity and security of your application. Flask provides various tools and techniques for implementing data validation, including request validation, form validation with Flask-WTF, and custom validation logic. By incorporating data validation into your Flask-based APIs, you can enhance the reliability, security, and user experience of your applications. Effective data validation is a critical aspect of building robust and trustworthy APIs that meet the needs of your users and stakeholders.

Techniques for Input Validation: Ensuring Data Integrity

Input validation is a fundamental aspect of API development, ensuring that the data received from clients meets specified criteria and quality standards. By validating input data, developers can prevent security vulnerabilities, data corruption, and inconsistencies in their applications. Flask, a lightweight Python web framework, offers various techniques and tools for implementing input validation in API development. In this guide, we'll explore techniques for input validation in Flask-based APIs, covering best practices and examples.

Why Input Validation Matters

Input validation serves several important purposes in API development:

1. Security: Validating input data helps prevent security vulnerabilities such as SQL injection, cross-site scripting (XSS), and injection attacks.

2. Data Integrity: Ensuring that input data meets specified constraints and formats helps maintain data integrity and consistency within the system.

3. User Experience: Providing feedback to users about invalid input helps improve the user experience by guiding them to provide correct input.

Common Techniques for Input Validation

There are several techniques for validating input data in APIs, including:

1. Type Checking: Verifying that data types match the expected types (e.g., strings, integers, booleans).

2. Format Validation: Ensuring that data adheres to specified formats (e.g., email addresses, phone numbers, dates).

3. Length and Range Validation: Checking the length or range of numeric values or strings.

4. Presence Validation: Verifying that required fields are present and not empty.

5. Custom Validation: Implementing custom validation logic for complex data validation requirements.

Implementing Input Validation in Flask

Flask provides various mechanisms for implementing input validation in your API, including request validation, form validation, and custom validation logic.

Request Validation

Flask allows developers to access request data and perform validation directly within route functions using Flask's request object.

Example: Request Validation

```python
from flask import Flask, request, jsonify

app = Flask(__name__)

@app.route('/user', methods=['POST'])
def create_user():
    data = request.json
    if not data.get('name'):
        return jsonify({'error': 'Name is required'}), 400
    # Validate other fields...
    return jsonify({'message': 'User created successfully'})

if __name__ == '__main__':
```

```
app.run(debug=True)
```

In this example, the `create_user()` function validates the presence of the 'name' field in the JSON request data. If the field is missing, it returns a JSON response with a 400 Bad Request error.

Form Validation

Flask-WTF, an extension for Flask, provides support for form validation using WTForms, a flexible form validation and rendering library for Python.

Example: Form Validation with Flask-WTF

```python
from flask import Flask, render_template
from flask_wtf import FlaskForm
from wtforms import StringField, SubmitField
from wtforms.validators import DataRequired
app = Flask(__name__)
app.config['SECRET_KEY'] = 'your_secret_key'
class UserForm(FlaskForm):
```

```python
    name = StringField('Name', validators=[DataRequired()])
    email = StringField('Email', validators=[DataRequired()])
    submit = SubmitField('Submit')

@app.route('/user', methods=['GET', 'POST'])
def create_user():
    form = UserForm()
    if form.validate_on_submit():
        # Process form data
        return 'User created successfully'
    return render_template('user_form.html', form=form)

if __name__ == '__main__':
    app.run(debug=True)
```

In this example, the `UserForm` class defines form fields with validators, such as `DataRequired()` for ensuring that fields are not empty. The `create_user()` function validates the form data upon submission and processes it if validation passes.

Custom Validation Logic

Flask allows developers to implement custom validation logic for complex data validation requirements using Python code within route functions.

Example: Custom Validation Logic

```python
from flask import Flask, request, jsonify

app = Flask(__name__)

def validate_email(email):
    # Custom email validation logic
    if '@' not in email:
        return False
    return True

@app.route('/user', methods=['POST'])
def create_user():
    data = request.json
    if not data.get('email') or not validate_email(data.get('email')):
        return jsonify({'error': 'Invalid email address'}), 400
```

```
    # Process other fields...

    return jsonify({'message': 'User created successfully'})

if __name__ == '__main__':
    app.run(debug=True)
```

In this example, the `validate_email()` function implements custom email validation logic, checking for the presence of the '@' symbol. The `create_user()` function uses this custom validation logic to validate the email address provided in the request data.

Input validation is essential for ensuring the integrity, security, and reliability of your API. Flask provides various techniques and tools for implementing input validation, including request validation, form validation with Flask-WTF, and custom validation logic. By incorporating input validation into your Flask-based APIs, you can enhance the robustness and usability of your applications. Effective input validation is a critical aspect of building high-quality APIs that meet the needs of your users and stakeholders.

Chapter 7

Testing Your Masterpiece - Building Confidence in Your API

The Importance of Testing: Why Unit Testing Matters

In the realm of web development, particularly with Flask—a micro web framework for Python—the importance of testing, especially unit testing, cannot be overstated. Unit testing plays a crucial role in ensuring the reliability, stability, and maintainability of Flask APIs. This article delves into the fundamentals of Flask API development and explores why unit testing is essential for creating robust and error-free applications.

Fundamentals of Flask API Development:

Flask is a lightweight and flexible micro-framework for building web applications in Python. It provides tools and libraries for handling HTTP requests, routing, and rendering templates, making it ideal for developing RESTful APIs. In Flask, APIs are typically structured around routes, which define the URL endpoints and the functions that handle incoming requests.

A basic Flask API consists of:

1. Routes: URL patterns that map to specific functions or resources.

2. Request Handling: Functions that process incoming HTTP requests and return appropriate responses.

3. Data Serialization: Converting data between Python objects and JSON for communication with clients.

4. Error Handling: Handling exceptions and returning meaningful error responses to clients.

5. Middleware: Optional components for intercepting and processing requests before they reach the route handler.

With these fundamental components in place, Flask APIs can perform a wide range of tasks, from serving static content to complex business logic and database interactions.

The Importance of Testing in Flask API Development:

Testing is an integral part of the software development lifecycle, and Flask applications are no exception. However, testing Flask APIs presents unique challenges due to their asynchronous nature and dependency on external resources such as databases and third-party services. Unit testing, which focuses on testing individual units of code in isolation, is particularly valuable in this context.

Here's why unit testing matters in Flask API development:

1. Ensuring Functionality: Unit tests verify that each endpoint and function in the API behaves as expected under different conditions. By testing individual units of code in isolation, developers can identify and fix bugs early in the development process.

```python
# Example unit test for a Flask route
import unittest
from myapp import app

class TestFlaskApp(unittest.TestCase):
    def test_hello_world(self):
        tester = app.test_client(self)
        response = tester.get('/hello')
        self.assertEqual(response.status_code, 200)
        self.assertEqual(response.data, b'Hello, World!')

if __name__ == '__main__':
    unittest.main()
```

2. Detecting Regression: As Flask applications evolve, new features and optimizations may inadvertently introduce bugs or break existing functionality. Unit tests act as a safety net, catching regressions before they reach production and ensuring that code changes do not disrupt the API's behavior.

```python
# Example unit test for a Flask function

def divide(a, b):
    return a / b

def test_divide():
    assert divide(4, 2) == 2
    assert divide(0, 5) == 0
    assert divide(3, 0) == float('inf')
```

3. Facilitating Refactoring: Refactoring is an essential part of software development, but it can be risky without adequate test coverage. Unit tests provide confidence when refactoring code, allowing developers to make changes with the assurance that existing functionality remains intact.

```python
# Example unit test for refactored Flask function
```

```python
def add(a, b):
    return a + b

def test_add():
    assert add(1, 2) == 3
    assert add(0, 0) == 0
    assert add(-1, 1) == 0
```

4. Improving Documentation: Unit tests serve as executable documentation for the API's behavior. By reading the tests, developers can gain insights into how each endpoint and function should be used and what results to expect, enhancing overall code comprehension and maintainability.

```python
# Example unit test for Flask endpoint documentation
def test_documentation():
    tester = app.test_client()
    response = tester.get('/documentation')
    assert response.status_code == 200
    assert 'API Documentation' in str(response.data)
```

```

**5. Supporting Continuous Integration and Deployment:** Unit tests form the foundation of continuous integration (CI) and continuous deployment (CD) pipelines, ensuring that code changes are thoroughly tested before being deployed to production environments. Automated testing reduces the risk of introducing bugs and accelerates the development cycle.

```python

# Example CI/CD configuration for Flask API

# .github/workflows/main.yml

name: CI

on:

　push:

　　branches: [ main ]

　pull_request:

　　branches: [ main ]

jobs:

　test:

　　runs-on: ubuntu-latest

```
steps:
  - uses: actions/checkout@v2
  - name: Set up Python
    uses: actions/setup-python@v2
    with:
      python-version: '3.x'
  - name: Install dependencies
    run: pip install -r requirements.txt
  - name: Run tests
    run: pytest
```

Unit testing is a fundamental practice in Flask API development, providing numerous benefits including ensuring functionality, detecting regression, facilitating refactoring, improving documentation, and supporting continuous integration and deployment. By incorporating unit tests into the development workflow, developers can create more reliable, maintainable, and scalable Flask applications that meet the needs of users and stakeholders.

Setting Up a Testing Framework: Tools for Flask API Development

In the world of Flask API development, having a robust testing framework in place is essential for ensuring the reliability and quality of your applications. A well-designed testing framework allows developers to verify the functionality of their endpoints, catch bugs early in the development process, and maintain code integrity over time. This article explores the tools and techniques for setting up a comprehensive testing framework for Flask API development.

Choosing the Right Tools:

When it comes to testing Flask APIs, developers have a variety of tools and libraries at their disposal. The choice of testing tools depends on factors such as project requirements, team preferences, and the complexity of the application. Here are some popular tools for setting up a testing framework for Flask API development:

1. pytest: pytest is a powerful testing framework for Python that offers a simple syntax, extensive plugin ecosystem, and support for various types of testing, including unit tests, functional tests, and integration tests. It integrates seamlessly with Flask and provides features such as fixtures, parameterized testing, and powerful assertions.

2. Flask-Testing: Flask-Testing is a Flask extension that simplifies the process of writing unit tests for Flask applications. It provides a TestCase class with built-in methods for making requests to Flask endpoints, managing application contexts, and handling database transactions. Flask-Testing is particularly useful for writing comprehensive unit tests that cover all aspects of your Flask API.

3. unittest: unittest is Python's built-in testing framework, inspired by JUnit. While it may not be as feature-rich as pytest, unittest is still a viable option for writing tests for Flask APIs, especially for developers who prefer a more structured approach to testing. unittest provides classes and methods for defining test cases, test suites, and assertions.

4. Mocking Libraries (e.g., unittest.mock): Mocking libraries such as unittest.mock are invaluable for writing unit tests that involve external dependencies, such as databases, third-party APIs, or external services. Mocking allows developers to simulate the behavior of these dependencies in a controlled environment, enabling thorough testing without relying on external resources.

Setting Up a Testing Environment:

Now that we've covered the tools available for testing Flask APIs, let's walk through the process of setting up a testing environment and writing tests for a simple Flask API. We'll use pytest and Flask-Testing for this example, as they provide a convenient and flexible framework for writing and running tests.

1. Installation: First, make sure you have Flask, pytest, and Flask-Testing installed in your development environment. You can install them via pip:

```
pip install Flask pytest Flask-Testing
```

2. Project Structure: Organize your Flask project with a directory structure that separates your application code from your tests. For example:

```
myapp/
├── app/
│   ├── __init__.py
│   ├── views.py
│   └── models.py
├── tests/
│   ├── __init__.py
│   └── test_views.py
└── run.py
```

```

**3. Writing Tests:** Create test modules within the "tests" directory and write test cases using pytest syntax. Here's an example of a simple test case for a Flask endpoint:

```python
# tests/test_views.py

from myapp import app

def test_hello_world():
    tester = app.test_client()
    response = tester.get('/hello')
    assert response.status_code == 200
    assert b'Hello, World!' in response.data
```

4. Running Tests: You can run your tests using the pytest command-line interface. Navigate to the root directory of your project and run:

```
pytest
```
```

pytest will discover and execute all test modules within the "tests" directory, displaying detailed output and summaries of test results.

Setting up a testing framework for Flask API development is a crucial step in ensuring the reliability, stability, and maintainability of your applications. By choosing the right tools, organizing your project structure effectively, and writing comprehensive tests, you can build confidence in your codebase and deliver high-quality Flask APIs that meet the needs of your users and stakeholders. Whether you prefer pytest, Flask-Testing, unittest, or a combination of these tools, investing in testing pays dividends in the long run by reducing bugs, improving code quality, and enabling faster iteration and deployment cycles.

Writing Unit Tests for Flask Applications: Ensuring Flawless Functionality

Unit testing is a critical aspect of Flask application development, ensuring that each component of your API functions correctly in isolation. By writing comprehensive unit tests, developers can catch bugs early, maintain code quality, and facilitate code refactoring. This article explores the fundamentals of writing unit tests for Flask applications, focusing on testing endpoints, handling exceptions, and mocking external dependencies.

Understanding Flask Application Structure:

Before diving into unit testing, it's essential to understand the structure of a typical Flask application.

A Flask application consists of:

1. Application Factory: A function that creates and configures the Flask application instance.

2. Blueprints: Modular components that define groups of related routes and views.

3. Views: Functions that handle incoming HTTP requests and return responses.

4. Models: Classes that represent data structures and interact with the database.

5. Templates: HTML files for rendering dynamic content using Jinja2 templating engine.

6. Static Files: CSS, JavaScript, and other static assets served by the application.

Unit Testing Flask Endpoints:

Endpoints are the backbone of a Flask API, defining the routes through which clients interact with the application. Writing unit tests for Flask endpoints involves verifying that each endpoint behaves as expected under different conditions. Here's an example of writing unit tests for a simple Flask endpoint:

```python
```

```python
# tests/test_endpoints.py
import unittest
from myapp import create_app

class TestEndpoints(unittest.TestCase):
    def setUp(self):
        self.app = create_app(testing=True)
        self.client = self.app.test_client()

    def test_hello_world(self):
        response = self.client.get('/hello')
        self.assertEqual(response.status_code, 200)
        self.assertEqual(response.data, b'Hello, World!')

    def test_missing_route(self):
        response = self.client.get('/missing')
        self.assertEqual(response.status_code, 404)

if __name__ == '__main__':
    unittest.main()
```

In this example, we define a test case class `TestEndpoints` with two test methods: `test_hello_world` and `test_missing_route`. We use the Flask test client to make requests to the `/hello` and `/missing` routes, asserting the expected status codes and response data.

Handling Exceptions in Flask Endpoints:

Flask applications often include error handling logic to handle exceptions gracefully and return meaningful error responses to clients. When writing unit tests for Flask endpoints, it's essential to verify that error-handling mechanisms function correctly. Here's an example of testing error handling in a Flask endpoint:

```python
# tests/test_error_handling.py

import unittest

from myapp import create_app

class TestErrorHandling(unittest.TestCase):
    def setUp(self):
        self.app = create_app(testing=True)
        self.client = self.app.test_client()

    def test_404_not_found(self):
```

```
        response = self.client.get('/not_found')

        self.assertEqual(response.status_code, 404)

        self.assertEqual(response.json['message'], 'Not Found')

    def test_500_internal_server_error(self):

        # Simulate internal server error by passing invalid data

        response = self.client.post('/error', json={})

        self.assertEqual(response.status_code, 500)

        self.assertEqual(response.json['message'], 'Internal Server Error')

if __name__ == '__main__':

    unittest.main()
```

In this example, we define a test case class `TestErrorHandling` with two test methods: `test_404_not_found` and `test_500_internal_server_error`. We use the Flask test client to make requests to endpoints that intentionally raise 404 and 500 errors, asserting the expected status codes and error messages.

Mocking External Dependencies:

Flask applications often rely on external dependencies such as databases, third-party APIs, or services. When writing unit tests for Flask applications, it's essential to isolate these external dependencies using mocking libraries such as `unittest.mock`. Here's an example of mocking external dependencies in a Flask endpoint test:

```python
# tests/test_external_dependencies.py

import unittest

from unittest.mock import patch

from myapp import create_app

class TestExternalDependencies(unittest.TestCase):

    def setUp(self):

        self.app = create_app(testing=True)

        self.client = self.app.test_client()

    @patch('myapp.views.external_api_call')

    def test_external_dependency(self, mock_external_api_call):

        mock_external_api_call.return_value = {'data': 'mocked_response'}

        response = self.client.get('/data')
```

```
        self.assertEqual(response.status_code, 200)

        self.assertEqual(response.json['data'],
'mocked_response')

if __name__ == '__main__':

    unittest.main()
```

In this example, we use the `@patch` decorator from the `unittest.mock` module to mock the `external_api_call` function imported in the Flask view. We then test the behavior of the endpoint `/data` when the external dependency is mocked, asserting the expected response data.

Writing unit tests for Flask applications is essential for ensuring flawless functionality, catching bugs early, and maintaining code quality. By testing endpoints, handling exceptions, and mocking external dependencies, developers can build confidence in their codebase and deliver reliable Flask APIs that meet the needs of users and stakeholders. Whether you're testing simple endpoints or complex business logic, investing in unit testing pays dividends in the long run by reducing bugs, improving code maintainability, and enabling faster iteration and deployment cycles.

Chapter 8

Building a Dynamic Weather App with Flask - Consuming External Data

Understanding Weather APIs: Accessing Real-Time Data

Weather APIs provide access to real-time weather data, enabling developers to incorporate weather information into their applications. In this tutorial, we'll delve into the fundamentals of weather APIs, focusing on accessing real-time weather data using Flask, a micro web framework for Python.

Understanding Weather APIs:

Weather APIs allow developers to retrieve weather data from various sources, such as meteorological organizations, weather stations, or third-party providers. These APIs typically provide data such as temperature, humidity, wind speed, and atmospheric pressure for a given location.

Some popular weather APIs include OpenWeatherMap, WeatherAPI, and AccuWeather. These APIs offer both free and paid plans, with varying levels of access and features.

Accessing Real-Time Data with Flask:

Flask is a lightweight and flexible framework for building web applications in Python. It provides tools and libraries for routing requests, handling HTTP methods, and rendering templates. Flask is well-suited for building RESTful APIs, making it an ideal choice for accessing real-time weather data.

Setting Up the Environment:

Before we begin, make sure you have Python and Flask installed on your system. You can install Flask using pip:

```bash
pip install Flask
```

Creating a Flask Application:

Let's create a simple Flask application to demonstrate how to access real-time weather data. We'll use the OpenWeatherMap API to retrieve weather information.

```python
from flask import Flask, jsonify
import requests

app = Flask(__name__)

@app.route('/weather/<city>')
```

```
def get_weather(city):

    api_key = 'YOUR_API_KEY'

    url = f'http://api.openweathermap.org/data/2.5/weather?q={city}&appid={api_key}&units=metric'

    response = requests.get(url)

    data = response.json()

    weather_data = {

        'temperature': data['main']['temp'],

        'humidity': data['main']['humidity'],

        'description': data['weather'][0]['description'],

        'wind_speed': data['wind']['speed']

    }

    return jsonify(weather_data)

if __name__ == '__main__':

    app.run(debug=True)
```

Replace 'YOUR_API_KEY' with your actual OpenWeatherMap API key. This code defines a Flask route '/weather/<city>' that accepts a city name as a parameter. It then makes a request to the OpenWeatherMap API to retrieve weather data for the specified city and returns the data as JSON.

Testing the API:

To test the API, run the Flask application and navigate to 'http://localhost:5000/weather/city_name' in your web browser, replacing 'city_name' with the name of the city you want to retrieve weather data for.

In this tutorial, we've explored the basics of accessing real-time weather data using Flask and a weather API. We've seen how to create a simple Flask application that retrieves weather information from the OpenWeatherMap API and returns it as JSON. With this knowledge, you can now integrate weather data into your own applications and projects.

Building a Flask API to Fetch Weather Information

In this tutorial, we will learn how to build a Flask API to fetch weather information using a weather API. Flask is a lightweight web framework for Python that is ideal for building APIs. We will use Flask to create endpoints that can be accessed to retrieve weather data for specific locations.

Understanding Flask Fundamentals for API Development:

Flask is a micro web framework for Python that allows developers to quickly build web applications and APIs. It provides tools for routing requests, handling HTTP methods, and rendering responses. Flask is lightweight, flexible, and easy to use, making it a popular choice for building APIs.

Setting Up the Environment:

Before we start building our Flask API, make sure you have Python and Flask installed on your system. You can install Flask using pip:

```bash
pip install Flask
```

Additionally, we will need to sign up for a weather API provider to fetch weather data. In this tutorial, we will use OpenWeatherMap as our weather API provider. Sign up for an account on their website and obtain an API key.

Building the Flask API:

Now, let's start building our Flask API to fetch weather information.

```python
from flask import Flask, request, jsonify
```

```python
import requests

app = Flask(__name__)

@app.route('/weather', methods=['GET'])
def get_weather():
    city = request.args.get('city')
    if not city:
        return jsonify({'error': 'City parameter is required'}), 400
    api_key = 'YOUR_API_KEY'
    url = f'http://api.openweathermap.org/data/2.5/weather?q={city}&appid={api_key}&units=metric'
    response = requests.get(url)
    if response.status_code != 200:
        return jsonify({'error': 'Failed to fetch weather data'}), 500
    data = response.json()
    weather_data = {
        'temperature': data['main']['temp'],
```

```
        'humidity': data['main']['humidity'],

        'description': data['weather'][0]['description'],

        'wind_speed': data['wind']['speed']

    }

    return jsonify(weather_data)

if __name__ == '__main__':

    app.run(debug=True)
```

Replace 'YOUR_API_KEY' with your actual OpenWeatherMap API key. This code defines a Flask route '/weather' that accepts a 'city' parameter as a query parameter. It then makes a request to the OpenWeatherMap API to retrieve weather data for the specified city and returns the data as JSON.

Testing the API:

To test the API, run the Flask application and make a GET request to 'http://localhost:5000/weather?city=city_name' in your browser or using a tool like Postman, replacing 'city_name' with the name of the city you want to fetch weather data for.

In this tutorial, we've learned how to build a Flask API to fetch weather information using a weather API. We've used Flask's routing and request handling capabilities to create an endpoint that accepts a city parameter and returns weather data for that city. With this knowledge, you can now build your own APIs to fetch weather information or integrate weather data into your existing applications.

Displaying Weather Data on a User Interface using Flask

In this tutorial, we'll expand upon our previous Flask API for fetching weather information and integrate it into a user interface. We'll use Flask to serve a simple web page that allows users to input a city name and fetch weather data for that city. We'll then display the retrieved weather data on the user interface.

Understanding Flask Fundamentals for API Development:

Flask is a lightweight web framework for Python that is ideal for building web applications and APIs. It provides tools for routing requests, handling HTTP methods, and rendering responses. Flask allows developers to create web applications quickly and easily.

Setting Up the Environment:

Before we start building our application, make sure you have Python and Flask installed on your system. You can install Flask using pip:

```bash
```

```
pip install Flask
```

Additionally, make sure you have obtained an API key from a weather API provider, such as OpenWeatherMap, to fetch weather data. We'll use the same Flask API we built in the previous tutorial to fetch weather information.

Building the Flask Application:

Now, let's start building our Flask application to display weather data on a user interface.

```python
from flask import Flask, render_template, request, jsonify

import requests

app = Flask(__name__)

@app.route('/')

def index():

    return render_template('index.html')

@app.route('/weather', methods=['POST'])

def get_weather():
```

```python
city = request.form['city']

if not city:

    return jsonify({'error': 'City parameter is required'}), 400

api_key = 'YOUR_API_KEY'

url = f'http://api.openweathermap.org/data/2.5/weather?q={city}&appid={api_key}&units=metric'

response = requests.get(url)

if response.status_code != 200:

    return jsonify({'error': 'Failed to fetch weather data'}), 500

data = response.json()

weather_data = {

    'temperature': data['main']['temp'],

    'humidity': data['main']['humidity'],

    'description': data['weather'][0]['description'],

    'wind_speed': data['wind']['speed']

}
```

```
    return render_template('weather.html', weather_data=weather_data)

if __name__ == '__main__':

    app.run(debug=True)
```

Replace 'YOUR_API_KEY' with your actual OpenWeatherMap API key. This code defines two routes - '/' for the homepage and '/weather' for fetching weather data. The homepage route renders an HTML template named 'index.html', which contains a form to input the city name. When the form is submitted, the '/weather' route is called via a POST request, which retrieves weather data for the specified city and renders an HTML template named 'weather.html', passing the weather data as a context variable.

Creating HTML Templates:

Now, let's create the HTML templates for our application.

index.html:

```html
<!DOCTYPE html>

<html>

<head>
```

```
    <title>Weather App</title>
</head>
<body>
    <h1>Weather App</h1>
    <form action="/weather" method="post">
        <label for="city">Enter City:</label>
        <input type="text" id="city" name="city" required>
        <button type="submit">Get Weather</button>
    </form>
</body>
</html>
```

weather.html:

```html
<!DOCTYPE html>
<html>
<head>
```

```
    <title>Weather Information</title>
  </head>
  <body>
    <h1>Weather Information</h1>
    <p>Temperature: {{ weather_data.temperature }} °C</p>
    <p>Humidity: {{ weather_data.humidity }}%</p>
    <p>Description: {{ weather_data.description }}</p>
    <p>Wind Speed: {{ weather_data.wind_speed }} m/s</p>
  </body>
</html>
```

Testing the Application:

To test the application, run the Flask application and navigate to 'http://localhost:5000' in your web browser. Enter the name of a city in the input field and click 'Get Weather'. The weather information for the specified city should be displayed on the page.

In this tutorial, we've learned how to build a Flask application to display weather data on a user interface.

We've used Flask's routing and rendering capabilities to create a simple web page with a form for inputting the city name. When the form is submitted, the application fetches weather data using the Flask API we built earlier and displays it on another page. With this knowledge, you can now build your own web applications to fetch and display weather information.

Chapter 9

Creating a Simple Social Media Platform - Connecting Users with Flask

Designing a User-Centric API: User Registration and Login with Flask

In this tutorial, we'll focus on designing a user-centric API that includes user registration and login functionalities using Flask, a micro web framework for Python. User registration and login are essential features for many web applications, allowing users to create accounts and access personalized content securely.

Understanding Flask Fundamentals for API Development:

Flask is a lightweight and flexible web framework for Python that provides tools for building web applications and APIs. It offers features such as routing, request handling, and response rendering, making it suitable for developing RESTful APIs. Flask allows developers to design APIs efficiently and easily.

Setting Up the Environment:

Before we begin, ensure you have Python and Flask installed on your system. You can install Flask using pip:

```bash
```

pip install Flask
```

We'll also use Flask SQLAlchemy for database operations, so install it as well:

```bash
pip install Flask-SQLAlchemy
```

Additionally, we'll use Werkzeug for password hashing, install it using pip:

```bash
pip install Werkzeug
```

Building the Flask Application:

Let's start building our Flask application to implement user registration and login functionalities.

```python
from flask import Flask, request, jsonify, make_response
from flask_sqlalchemy import SQLAlchemy

```python
from werkzeug.security import generate_password_hash, check_password_hash

import jwt

import datetime

app = Flask(__name__)

app.config['SECRET_KEY'] = 'your_secret_key'

app.config['SQLALCHEMY_DATABASE_URI'] = 'sqlite:///users.db'

db = SQLAlchemy(app)

class User(db.Model):

    id = db.Column(db.Integer, primary_key=True)

    username = db.Column(db.String(50), unique=True, nullable=False)

    email = db.Column(db.String(50), unique=True, nullable=False)

    password = db.Column(db.String(100), nullable=False)

@app.route('/register', methods=['POST'])

def register():

    data = request.get_json()
```

```python
    hashed_password = generate_password_hash(data['password'], method='sha256')

    new_user = User(username=data['username'], email=data['email'], password=hashed_password)

    db.session.add(new_user)

    db.session.commit()

    return jsonify({'message': 'User registered successfully'}), 201

@app.route('/login', methods=['POST'])

def login():

    auth = request.authorization

    if not auth or not auth.username or not auth.password:

        return make_response('Could not verify', 401, {'WWW-Authenticate': 'Basic realm="Login required!"'})

    user = User.query.filter_by(username=auth.username).first()

    if not user:

        return make_response('Could not verify', 401, {'WWW-Authenticate': 'Basic realm="Login required!"'})
```

```
        if check_password_hash(user.password,
auth.password):

            token = jwt.encode({'user_id': user.id, 'exp':
datetime.datetime.utcnow() +
datetime.timedelta(minutes=30)},
app.config['SECRET_KEY'])

            return jsonify({'token': token.decode('UTF-8')})

        return make_response('Could not verify', 401,
{'WWW-Authenticate': 'Basic realm="Login
required!"'})

if __name__ == '__main__':

    db.create_all()

    app.run(debug=True)
```
```

This code defines a Flask application with two routes: '/register' for user registration and '/login' for user login. We use SQLAlchemy to interact with the SQLite database to store user information securely. We also use Werkzeug for password hashing and JWT (JSON Web Tokens) for authentication.

**User Registration:**

To register a new user, send a POST request to '/register' with JSON data containing 'username', 'email', and
```

'password'. The password is hashed before storing it in the database.

User Login:

To log in, send a POST request to '/login' with HTTP Basic Authentication. If the credentials are valid, a JWT token is generated and returned as a response.

Testing the API:

To test the API, you can use tools like Postman or cURL. Here's an example of how to register a new user and then log in:

1. Register a new user:

```bash
curl -X POST -H "Content-Type: application/json" -d '{"username":"user1", "email":"user1@example.com", "password":"password123"}' http://localhost:5000/register
```

Response: {"message": "User registered successfully"}

2. Log in with the registered user:

```bash
curl -u user1:password123 -X POST http://localhost:5000/login
```

```

Response: {"token":
"eyJ0eXAiOiJKV1QiLCJhbGciOiJIUzI1NiJ9.eyJ1c2Vy
X2lkIjoxLCJleHAiOjE2MjIxNTYzNjd9.6l3AnL6omO_
tUgG4vAIqHf7dRreXf4pKbOwHhSjUuX8"}

The token returned in the login response can be used for authentication in subsequent requests by including it in the Authorization header as a Bearer token.

In this tutorial, we've designed a user-centric API with user registration and login functionalities using Flask. We've leveraged Flask's capabilities for routing, request handling, and response rendering, along with Flask SQLAlchemy for database operations and Werkzeug for password hashing. With this API, users can register for an account, securely store their credentials, and log in to access protected resources. This tutorial provides a solid foundation for building user authentication systems in Flask-based web applications.

## Building Endpoints for User Interaction: Posting and Sharing Content with Flask

In this tutorial, we'll extend our Flask API to include endpoints for users to post and share content. Posting and sharing functionalities are common in social media platforms and community-driven websites, allowing users to create and distribute their content. By implementing these endpoints, we'll enable users to interact with our API by creating and sharing posts.
```

Understanding Flask Fundamentals for API Development:

Flask is a lightweight and flexible web framework for Python that provides tools for building web applications and APIs. It offers features such as routing, request handling, and response rendering, making it suitable for developing RESTful APIs. Flask allows developers to design APIs efficiently and easily.

Setting Up the Environment:

Before we begin, ensure you have Python and Flask installed on your system. You can install Flask using pip:

```bash
pip install Flask
```

Additionally, we'll use Flask SQLAlchemy for database operations, so install it as well:

```bash
pip install Flask-SQLAlchemy
```

Building the Flask Application:

Let's start building our Flask application to implement posting and sharing functionalities.

```python
from flask import Flask, request, jsonify

from flask_sqlalchemy import SQLAlchemy

app = Flask(__name__)

app.config['SQLALCHEMY_DATABASE_URI'] = 'sqlite:///posts.db'

db = SQLAlchemy(app)

class Post(db.Model):

    id = db.Column(db.Integer, primary_key=True)

    title = db.Column(db.String(100), nullable=False)

    content = db.Column(db.Text, nullable=False)

    author = db.Column(db.String(50), nullable=False)

@app.route('/posts', methods=['GET'])

def get_posts():

    posts = Post.query.all()

    output = []

    for post in posts:
```

```
    post_data = {'id': post.id, 'title': post.title, 'content': post.content, 'author': post.author}

    output.append(post_data)

  return jsonify({'posts': output})

@app.route('/posts', methods=['POST'])

def create_post():

  data = request.get_json()

  new_post = Post(title=data['title'], content=data['content'], author=data['author'])

  db.session.add(new_post)

  db.session.commit()

  return jsonify({'message': 'Post created successfully'}), 201

if __name__ == '__main__':

  db.create_all()

  app.run(debug=True)
```
```

This code defines a Flask application with two routes: '/posts' for retrieving posts and creating new posts. We
```

use SQLAlchemy to interact with the SQLite database to store post information securely.

Retrieving Posts:

To retrieve posts, send a GET request to '/posts'. This endpoint returns a JSON response containing a list of all posts available in the database.

Creating Posts:

To create a new post, send a POST request to '/posts' with JSON data containing 'title', 'content', and 'author' fields. The new post is added to the database upon successful creation.

Testing the API:

To test the API, you can use tools like Postman or cURL. Here's an example of how to retrieve posts and create a new post:

1. Retrieve posts:

```bash

curl -X GET http://localhost:5000/posts

```

Response: {"posts": []} (No posts initially)

2. Create a new post:

```bash
curl -X POST -H "Content-Type: application/json" -d '{"title":"First Post", "content":"This is my first post!", "author":"John"}' http://localhost:5000/posts
```

Response: {"message": "Post created successfully"}

3. Retrieve posts again:

```bash
curl -X GET http://localhost:5000/posts
```

Response: {"posts": [{"id": 1, "title": "First Post", "content": "This is my first post!", "author": "John"}]}

In this tutorial, we've built endpoints for user interaction, allowing users to post and share content using our Flask API. We've leveraged Flask's capabilities for routing, request handling, and response rendering, along with Flask SQLAlchemy for database operations. With these endpoints, users can now create and share their content, providing a foundation for building more advanced features in web applications and APIs.

Exploring Authentication Techniques: Securing Your Social Network with Flask

In this tutorial, we'll dive into authentication techniques to secure a social network built with Flask. Authentication is crucial for protecting user accounts and sensitive data in web applications. By implementing authentication mechanisms, we can ensure that only authorized users can access certain resources and perform specific actions within our application.

Understanding Flask Fundamentals for API Development:

Flask is a lightweight and flexible web framework for Python that provides tools for building web applications and APIs. It offers features such as routing, request handling, and response rendering, making it suitable for developing RESTful APIs. Flask allows developers to design APIs efficiently and easily.

Setting Up the Environment:

Before we begin, ensure you have Python and Flask installed on your system. You can install Flask using pip:

```bash

pip install Flask

```

We'll also use Flask SQLAlchemy for database operations, so install it as well:

```bash
pip install Flask-SQLAlchemy
```

Additionally, we'll use Werkzeug for password hashing and JWT (JSON Web Tokens) for authentication, install them using pip:

```bash
pip install Werkzeug
pip install PyJWT
```

Building the Flask Application:

Let's start building our Flask application to implement authentication mechanisms for our social network.

```python
from flask import Flask, request, jsonify, make_response
from flask_sqlalchemy import SQLAlchemy
from werkzeug.security import generate_password_hash, check_password_hash
```

```python
import jwt

import datetime

app = Flask(__name__)

app.config['SECRET_KEY'] = 'your_secret_key'

app.config['SQLALCHEMY_DATABASE_URI'] = 'sqlite:///users.db'

db = SQLAlchemy(app)

class User(db.Model):
    id = db.Column(db.Integer, primary_key=True)
    username = db.Column(db.String(50), unique=True, nullable=False)
    email = db.Column(db.String(50), unique=True, nullable=False)
    password = db.Column(db.String(100), nullable=False)

@app.route('/register', methods=['POST'])
def register():
    data = request.get_json()
```

```python
    hashed_password = generate_password_hash(data['password'], method='sha256')

    new_user = User(username=data['username'], email=data['email'], password=hashed_password)

    db.session.add(new_user)

    db.session.commit()

    return jsonify({'message': 'User registered successfully'}), 201

@app.route('/login', methods=['POST'])
def login():

    auth = request.authorization

    if not auth or not auth.username or not auth.password:

        return make_response('Could not verify', 401, {'WWW-Authenticate': 'Basic realm="Login required!"'})

    user = User.query.filter_by(username=auth.username).first()

    if not user:

        return make_response('Could not verify', 401, {'WWW-Authenticate': 'Basic realm="Login required!"'})
```

```python
    if check_password_hash(user.password, auth.password):

        token = jwt.encode({'user_id': user.id, 'exp': datetime.datetime.utcnow() + datetime.timedelta(minutes=30)}, app.config['SECRET_KEY'])

        return jsonify({'token': token.decode('UTF-8')})

    return make_response('Could not verify', 401, {'WWW-Authenticate': 'Basic realm="Login required!"'})

@app.route('/protected', methods=['GET'])

def protected():

    token = request.headers.get('Authorization')

    if not token:

        return jsonify({'error': 'Token is missing'}), 401

    try:

        data = jwt.decode(token.split()[1], app.config['SECRET_KEY'], algorithms=['HS256'])

        user = User.query.get(data['user_id'])

        return jsonify({'message': f'Welcome {user.username}! This is a protected route.'})
```

```
except jwt.ExpiredSignatureError:

    return jsonify({'error': 'Token has expired'}), 401

except jwt.InvalidTokenError:

    return jsonify({'error': 'Invalid token'}), 401

if __name__ == '__main__':

    db.create_all()

    app.run(debug=True)
```

This code defines a Flask application with three routes: '/register' for user registration, '/login' for user login, and '/protected' as a protected route that requires authentication. We use SQLAlchemy to interact with the SQLite database to store user information securely. We also use Werkzeug for password hashing and JWT for authentication.

User Registration and Login:

Users can register for an account by sending a POST request to '/register' with JSON data containing 'username', 'email', and 'password'. They can then log in using the '/login' endpoint with HTTP Basic Authentication.

Protected Route:

The '/protected' route is a protected endpoint that requires authentication. Users must include a valid JWT token in the Authorization header to access this route. If the token is valid and not expired, the user is granted access to the protected resource.

Testing the API:

To test the API, you can use tools like Postman or cURL. Here's an example of how to register a new user, log in, and access the protected route:

1. Register a new user:

```bash
curl -X POST -H "Content-Type: application/json" -d '{"username":"user1", "email":"user1@example.com", "password":"password123"}' http://localhost:5000/register
```

Response: {"message": "User registered successfully"}

2. Log in with the registered user:

```bash
curl -u user1:password123 -X POST http://localhost:5000/login
```

Response: {"token": "eyJ0eXAiOiJKV1QiLCJhbGciOiJIUzI1NiJ9.eyJ1c2Vy X2lkIjoxLCJleHAiOjE2MjIxNTYzNjd9.6l3AnL6omO_ tUgG4vAIqHf7dRreXf4pKbOwHhSjUuX8"}

3. Access the protected route with the obtained token:

```bash

curl -H "Authorization: Bearer eyJ0eXAiOiJKV1QiLCJhbGciOiJIUzI1NiJ9.eyJ1c2Vy X2lkIjoxLCJleHAiOjE2MjIxNTYzNjd9.6l3AnL6omO_ tUgG4vAIqHf7dRreXf4pKbOwHhSjUuX8" http://localhost:5000/protected

```

Response: {"message": "Welcome user1! This is a protected route."}

In this tutorial, we've explored authentication techniques to secure a social network built with Flask. We've implemented user registration and login functionalities, as well as a protected route that requires authentication using JWT tokens. With these authentication mechanisms in place, we can ensure the security of our application and protect user accounts and sensitive data.

Chapter 10

Deployment Strategies - Sharing Your API with the World

Choosing the Right Deployment Environment: Cloud or On-Premises for Flask API Development

When deciding where to deploy your Flask API, you must weigh the benefits and considerations of deploying in the cloud versus on-premises. Both deployment environments have their advantages and trade-offs, and the decision depends on factors such as scalability, cost, security, and infrastructure management preferences. In this tutorial, we'll explore the pros and cons of each deployment option and provide guidance on choosing the right environment for your Flask API.

Understanding Flask Fundamentals for API Development:

Before delving into deployment considerations, let's review the basics of Flask for API development. Flask is a lightweight and flexible web framework for Python that provides tools for building web applications and APIs. It offers features such as routing, request handling, and response rendering, making it suitable for developing RESTful APIs. Flask enables developers to design APIs efficiently and easily.

Cloud Deployment:

Cloud deployment involves hosting the Flask API on a cloud platform, such as Amazon Web Services (AWS), Google Cloud Platform (GCP), or Microsoft Azure. Cloud providers offer a range of services and features tailored to deploying web applications and APIs, including managed infrastructure, auto-scaling, monitoring, and security features.

Pros of Cloud Deployment:

1. Scalability: Cloud platforms provide auto-scaling capabilities, allowing your Flask API to handle varying levels of traffic automatically. This ensures that your API remains responsive and available, even during periods of high demand.

2. Flexibility: Cloud platforms offer a wide range of services and resources that can be easily integrated into your Flask API deployment, such as databases, caching services, and content delivery networks (CDNs). You can leverage these services to enhance the functionality and performance of your API.

3. Managed Services: Cloud providers offer managed services for deploying and managing web applications and APIs, reducing the operational burden on developers. This includes services such as container orchestration (e.g., AWS Elastic Container Service, Google Kubernetes Engine), serverless computing (e.g., AWS Lambda, Google Cloud Functions), and managed database services (e.g., Amazon RDS, Google Cloud SQL).

4. Cost-Effectiveness: Cloud deployment can be cost-effective, especially for small to medium-sized projects, as it eliminates the need for upfront hardware investments and allows you to pay only for the resources you use on a pay-as-you-go basis.

Cons of Cloud Deployment:

1. Vendor Lock-in: Cloud deployment may lead to vendor lock-in, as you become dependent on the specific services and features provided by the chosen cloud provider. Migrating away from a cloud platform can be challenging and may require significant effort and resources.

2. Security Concerns: Storing sensitive data and hosting applications in the cloud raises security concerns, as it involves entrusting your data to a third-party provider. It's essential to implement robust security measures, such as encryption, access controls, and compliance certifications, to protect your Flask API and data from security threats.

On-Premises Deployment:

On-premises deployment involves hosting the Flask API on servers located within your organization's physical premises, such as a data center or server room. With on-premises deployment, you have full control over the infrastructure and resources used to host your API.

Pros of On-Premises Deployment:

1. Control and Customization: On-premises deployment gives you complete control over the hardware, software, and network infrastructure used to host your Flask API. You can customize the environment to meet specific requirements, optimize performance, and adhere to regulatory compliance standards.

2. Data Sovereignty: Hosting your Flask API on-premises allows you to maintain full control and ownership of your data, ensuring compliance with data privacy regulations and addressing concerns about data sovereignty and jurisdiction.

3. Security and Compliance: On-premises deployment provides greater control over security measures, allowing you to implement custom security policies, encryption techniques, and access controls to protect your Flask API and sensitive data. This can be particularly important for organizations operating in highly regulated industries, such as healthcare, finance, or government.

Cons of On-Premises Deployment:

1. Infrastructure Costs: On-premises deployment requires upfront investment in hardware, networking equipment, and infrastructure maintenance, including power, cooling, and physical security measures. These costs can be substantial, especially for large-scale deployments or organizations with limited IT budgets.

2. Scalability Challenges: On-premises deployment may face scalability challenges, as it may be difficult to rapidly scale resources to accommodate growing traffic or changing workload demands. Scaling hardware and infrastructure requires careful planning, procurement, and provisioning, which can lead to longer lead times and increased operational complexity.

3. Maintenance and Upkeep: On-premises deployment entails ongoing maintenance and upkeep of hardware, software, and infrastructure components, including hardware upgrades, software patches, and security updates. This requires dedicated IT staff and resources to ensure the reliability, performance, and security of the Flask API deployment.

When choosing between cloud and on-premises deployment for your Flask API, consider factors such as scalability, cost, security, control, and compliance requirements. Cloud deployment offers scalability, flexibility, and managed services, making it an attractive option for many projects, especially those with variable workloads and limited upfront investment capabilities. On the other hand, on-premises deployment provides greater control, customization, and data sovereignty, making it suitable for organizations with strict security and compliance requirements or specialized infrastructure needs. Ultimately, the decision depends on your specific project requirements, organizational goals, and resource constraints. By carefully evaluating the pros and cons of each deployment option, you can make an informed decision that best aligns with your objectives and constraints.

Configuration for Deployment: Optimizing Your API for Production with Flask

Deploying a Flask API to production involves more than just copying your development code to a server. It requires careful configuration and optimization to ensure reliability, scalability, and performance under real-world conditions. In this tutorial, we'll explore the key configuration steps for deploying a Flask API to production, including environment setup, security considerations, performance optimization, and best practices for managing configurations.

Understanding Flask Fundamentals for API Development:

Before diving into deployment configuration, let's review the fundamentals of Flask for API development. Flask is a lightweight and flexible web framework for Python that provides tools for building web applications and APIs. It offers features such as routing, request handling, and response rendering, making it suitable for developing RESTful APIs. Flask enables developers to design APIs efficiently and easily.

Setting Up the Environment:

1. Environment Variables: Use environment variables to manage configuration settings such as database connections, API keys, and environment-specific parameters. Flask provides the `os.environ` module to access environment variables within your application.

```python
import os

# Get environment variables
database_url = os.environ.get('DATABASE_URL')
api_key = os.environ.get('API_KEY')
```

2. Configuration Files: Store environment-specific configuration settings in separate configuration files, such as `config.py` for development settings and `config_prod.py` for production settings. Use the `app.config.from_pyfile()` method to load configuration settings from a file.

```python
# Load configuration from file
app.config.from_pyfile('config_prod.py')
```

Security Considerations:

1. Secret Key: Generate a secret key for securing session cookies and other cryptographic operations.

Keep the secret key secret and avoid hardcoding it in your source code. Use the `os.urandom()` function to generate a random secret key.

```python
# Generate a random secret key
app.secret_key = os.urandom(24)
```

2. HTTPS: Enable HTTPS (HTTP Secure) to encrypt communication between clients and the server, ensuring data privacy and security. Use a web server or reverse proxy (e.g., Nginx, Apache) to terminate SSL/TLS connections and forward requests to your Flask API over HTTPS.

Performance Optimization:

1. WSGI Server: Use a production-ready WSGI (Web Server Gateway Interface) server, such as Gunicorn or uWSGI, to serve your Flask API in production. WSGI servers are optimized for handling concurrent requests and can improve the performance and scalability of your application.

```bash
# Install Gunicorn
pip install gunicorn
```

```

**2. Middleware:** Utilize middleware components, such as Flask-Caching or Flask-Compress, to cache responses, compress data, and optimize performance. Middleware can reduce response times and bandwidth usage, resulting in faster API performance.

```python

# Example: Enable response compression with Flask-Compress

from flask_compress import Compress

compress = Compress()

compress.init_app(app)

```

Best Practices for Managing Configurations:

1. Separate Configuration Settings: Keep development, testing, and production configurations separate to ensure consistency and prevent accidental configuration leaks or overrides.

2. Environment-specific Overrides: Use environment-specific configuration files or environment variables to override default settings based on the deployment environment.
```

3. Version Control: Store configuration files in version control systems (e.g., Git) and follow best practices for managing secrets, such as using encrypted files or environment-specific configuration overrides.

Optimizing your Flask API for production deployment requires careful configuration and consideration of factors such as security, performance, and environment-specific settings. By following best practices for managing configurations, securing sensitive information, and optimizing performance, you can ensure that your Flask API operates reliably and efficiently in a production environment. Remember to test your deployment configuration thoroughly to identify and address any potential issues before going live. With proper configuration and optimization, your Flask API can deliver a seamless and secure experience for your users.

Monitoring and Maintaining Your API: Keeping Your Creation Alive with Flask

Once your Flask API is deployed to production, it's crucial to monitor and maintain it to ensure optimal performance, reliability, and availability. Monitoring allows you to track key metrics, detect issues, and respond to incidents promptly, while maintenance involves regular updates, optimizations, and bug fixes to keep your API running smoothly. In this tutorial, we'll explore strategies for monitoring and maintaining your Flask API, including logging, error handling, performance optimization, and automated testing.

Understanding Flask Fundamentals for API Development:

Before diving into monitoring and maintenance, let's review the fundamentals of Flask for API development. Flask is a lightweight and flexible web framework for Python that provides tools for building web applications and APIs. It offers features such as routing, request handling, and response rendering, making it suitable for developing RESTful APIs. Flask enables developers to design APIs efficiently and easily.

<u>Logging</u>:

Logging is essential for monitoring the behavior of your Flask API and diagnosing issues. Flask provides built-in support for logging through the `logging` module, allowing you to record important events, errors, and warnings.

```python
import logging

# Configure logging
logging.basicConfig(filename='api.log', level=logging.INFO)

# Log an info message
logging.info('API started successfully')

# Log an error message
```

```
try:
    # Code that may raise an error
    pass
except Exception as e:
    logging.error(f'An error occurred: {str(e)}')
```

You can customize the logging configuration to control the log format, output destination, and log level based on your requirements.

Error Handling:

Proper error handling is crucial for handling unexpected conditions and preventing API failures. Flask provides mechanisms for defining custom error handlers to handle different types of errors gracefully and return informative error responses to clients.

```python
from flask import Flask, jsonify

app = Flask(__name__)

# Custom error handler for 404 Not Found errors
@app.errorhandler(404)
```

```python
def not_found_error(error):
    return jsonify({'error': 'Not found'}), 404

# Custom error handler for 500 Internal Server Error
@app.errorhandler(500)
def internal_server_error(error):
    return jsonify({'error': 'Internal server error'}), 500
```

Performance Optimization:

Optimizing the performance of your Flask API is essential for ensuring fast response times and efficient resource utilization. Strategies for performance optimization include:

1. Caching: Use caching mechanisms, such as Flask-Caching or Redis, to cache responses and reduce database queries and processing overhead.

```python
from flask_caching import Cache

cache = Cache()

# Example: Enable response caching with Flask-Caching
cache.init_app(app)
```

```

**2. Database Optimization:** Optimize database queries, indexes, and schema design to improve query performance and reduce latency.

**3. Asynchronous Processing:** Use asynchronous programming techniques, such as async/await or Celery, to offload long-running tasks and improve request handling concurrency.

**Automated Testing:**

Automated testing is essential for detecting regressions, ensuring code quality, and validating API behavior across different environments. Flask supports various testing frameworks, such as pytest, unittest, and Flask-Testing, for writing and running automated tests.

```python
import pytest

# Example: Writing a test case with pytest
def test_get_user():
    response = app.test_client().get('/users/1')
    assert response.status_code == 200
    assert response.json['username'] == 'user1'
```
```

You can write unit tests, integration tests, and end-to-end tests to cover different aspects of your Flask API, including routing, request handling, data validation, and error handling.

Monitoring:

Monitoring involves tracking key metrics, such as response times, error rates, and server health, to detect anomalies and performance issues proactively. You can use monitoring tools and services, such as Prometheus, Grafana, or New Relic, to collect and visualize metrics and set up alerts for critical events.

```python
from prometheus_flask_exporter import PrometheusMetrics

metrics = PrometheusMetrics(app)

# Example: Exporting custom metrics with PrometheusMetrics

@metrics.do_not_track()
@app.route('/health')
def health_check():
    return 'OK', 200
```

By exporting custom metrics and integrating with monitoring systems, you can gain insights into the performance and health of your Flask API and take proactive measures to address issues and optimize performance.

Monitoring and maintaining your Flask API are essential tasks for ensuring its reliability, availability, and performance in production environments. By implementing logging, error handling, performance optimization, automated testing, and monitoring strategies, you can keep your API running smoothly and respond to incidents effectively. Remember to continuously monitor and analyze key metrics, perform regular maintenance tasks, and stay proactive in addressing issues and optimizing performance to provide a seamless experience for your users. With proper monitoring and maintenance, you can keep your Flask API alive and thriving in the ever-changing landscape of web development.

Conclusion

In conclusion, Flask is a powerful and versatile framework for building web applications and APIs with Python. Throughout this journey, we've explored the fundamentals of Flask API development, from routing and request handling to error handling, performance optimization, and deployment considerations.

Flask's simplicity and flexibility make it an excellent choice for developers of all skill levels to create APIs that are efficient, scalable, and maintainable. By leveraging Flask's features such as route decorators, request context, and response rendering, developers can design APIs that meet the specific requirements of their projects.

However, building a Flask API is just the beginning. Deploying and maintaining the API in production requires careful planning, configuration, monitoring, and maintenance. Whether deploying to the cloud or on-premises, developers must consider factors such as scalability, security, cost, and performance optimization to ensure the API's reliability and availability.

Logging and error handling play a crucial role in diagnosing issues and providing informative feedback to clients, while performance optimization techniques such as caching, database optimization, and asynchronous processing help to improve response times and resource utilization.

Automated testing is essential for detecting regressions and validating API behavior, ensuring that changes and updates do not introduce unintended side effects or break existing functionality.

Monitoring is another critical aspect of maintaining a Flask API, allowing developers to track key metrics, detect anomalies, and respond to incidents proactively. By integrating monitoring tools and services, developers can gain insights into the API's performance and health, enabling them to optimize performance and address issues promptly.

In essence, Flask API development is a journey of continuous learning and improvement. Whether you're a beginner exploring Flask for the first time or an experienced developer building complex APIs, there's always something new to discover and explore.

With its vibrant community, extensive documentation, and rich ecosystem of extensions and libraries, Flask empowers developers to create innovative and scalable APIs that drive value for businesses and users alike.

So, as you embark on your Flask API development journey, remember to embrace the fundamentals, experiment with new features and techniques, and never stop learning. With Flask as your companion, the possibilities are endless, and the adventure awaits. Happy coding!

Appendix

Exploring Common Flask Libraries and Extensions for API Development

Flask is a powerful web framework for building web applications and APIs with Python. While Flask provides the core functionality for creating routes, handling requests, and generating responses, its extensibility allows developers to enhance and extend its capabilities through libraries and extensions. In this tutorial, we'll explore some of the most commonly used Flask libraries and extensions for API development, covering authentication, database integration, serialization, validation, and more.

1. Flask-RESTful:

Flask-RESTful is an extension for Flask that adds support for building RESTful APIs quickly and easily. It provides tools for defining resources, handling requests, and generating responses in a RESTful manner.

```python
from flask import Flask

from flask_restful import Api, Resource

app = Flask(__name__)

api = Api(app)
```

```
class HelloWorld(Resource):

    def get(self):

        return {'hello': 'world'}

api.add_resource(HelloWorld, '/')

if __name__ == '__main__':

    app.run(debug=True)
```

With Flask-RESTful, you can define resources as classes and specify HTTP methods (GET, POST, PUT, DELETE) to handle different types of requests. It also supports request parsing, input validation, error handling, and content negotiation out of the box.

2. Flask-SQLAlchemy:

Flask-SQLAlchemy is a Flask extension that provides integration with SQLAlchemy, a powerful SQL toolkit and Object-Relational Mapping (ORM) library for Python. It simplifies database operations and allows developers to interact with databases using Python objects.

```python
from flask import Flask

from flask_sqlalchemy import SQLAlchemy
```

```python
app = Flask(__name__)

app.config['SQLALCHEMY_DATABASE_URI'] = 'sqlite:///app.db'

db = SQLAlchemy(app)

class User(db.Model):
    id = db.Column(db.Integer, primary_key=True)
    username = db.Column(db.String(80), unique=True, nullable=False)

    def __repr__(self):
        return '<User %r>' % self.username

if __name__ == '__main__':
    app.run(debug=True)
```

With Flask-SQLAlchemy, you can define database models as Python classes and perform database operations, such as querying, inserting, updating, and deleting records, using SQLAlchemy's expressive ORM syntax.

3. Flask-JWT-Extended:

Flask-JWT-Extended is an extension for Flask that adds support for JSON Web Tokens (JWT) authentication and authorization. It provides tools for generating, verifying, and decoding JWT tokens, allowing developers to secure their APIs with token-based authentication.

```python
from flask import Flask

from flask_jwt_extended import JWTManager, jwt_required, create_access_token

app = Flask(__name__)

app.config['JWT_SECRET_KEY'] = 'super-secret' # Change this!

jwt = JWTManager(app)

@app.route('/login', methods=['POST'])

def login():

    # Authenticate user

    access_token = create_access_token(identity='user')

    return {'access_token': access_token}

@app.route('/protected', methods=['GET'])

@jwt_required()

def protected():
```

```python
    return {'message': 'protected endpoint'}

if __name__ == '__main__':
    app.run(debug=True)
```

With Flask-JWT-Extended, you can protect routes by adding the `@jwt_required()` decorator, which verifies the JWT token included in the request headers. It also supports customizing token expiration, token refreshing, and token revocation.

4. Flask-Marshmallow:

Flask-Marshmallow is a Flask extension that integrates with the Marshmallow library, a powerful serialization and validation library for Python. It provides tools for serializing and deserializing complex data structures, validating input data, and generating consistent API responses.

```python
from flask import Flask

from flask_marshmallow import Marshmallow

app = Flask(__name__)

ma = Marshmallow(app)

class UserSchema(ma.Schema):
```

```
    class Meta:
        fields = ('id', 'username')
user_schema = UserSchema()
users_schema = UserSchema(many=True)
if __name__ == '__main__':
    app.run(debug=True)
```

With Flask-Marshmallow, you can define serialization schemas as classes and specify fields to include or exclude in the serialized output. It also supports data validation, error handling, and customizing serialization behavior.

5. Flask-CORS:

Flask-CORS is a Flask extension that adds Cross-Origin Resource Sharing (CORS) support to Flask applications, allowing them to interact with resources from different origins. It provides tools for configuring CORS policies, handling preflight requests, and enforcing cross-origin restrictions.

```python
from flask import Flask
from flask_cors import CORS
```

```
app = Flask(__name__)

CORS(app)

@app.route('/')

def index():

    return 'Hello, CORS enabled world!'

if __name__ == '__main__':

    app.run(debug=True)
```
```

With Flask-CORS, you can specify CORS headers, such as allowed origins, methods, headers, and credentials, to control access to your API from web clients running in different domains.

Flask's extensibility and ecosystem of libraries and extensions make it a versatile framework for building APIs with Python. By leveraging common Flask libraries and extensions such as Flask-RESTful, Flask-SQLAlchemy, Flask-JWT-Extended, Flask-Marshmallow, and Flask-CORS, developers can enhance their APIs with features such as RESTful routing, database integration, authentication, serialization, validation, and cross-origin support. These libraries and extensions provide tools and abstractions that streamline API development, improve code maintainability, and enhance overall developer productivity. Whether you're
```

building a simple CRUD API or a complex web application, Flask's rich ecosystem of extensions has you covered, allowing you to focus on delivering value to your users without reinventing the wheel.

www.ingramcontent.com/pod-product-compliance
Lightning Source LLC
Chambersburg PA
CBHW031619210526
45464CB00004B/1661